1 THESSALONIANS
2 THESSALONIANS
PHILIPPIANS
PHILEMON

Ernest W. Saunders

KNOX PREACHING GUIDES
John H. Hayes, Editor

John Knox Press
ATLANTA

Library of Congress Cataloging in Publication Data

Saunders, Ernest W.
   1 Thessalonians, 2 Thessalonians, Philippians,
Philemon.

   (Knox preaching guides)
   Bibliography: p.
   1. Bible. N.T. Thessalonians—Commentaries.
2. Bible. N.T. Philippians—Commentaries.
3. Bible. N.T. Philemon—Commentaries. I. Title.
II. Series.
BS2725.3.S27   227′.8   80-84657
ISBN 0-8042-3241-5 (pbk.)   AACR2

© copyright John Knox Press 1981
10 9 8 7 6 5 4 3 2 1
Printed in the United States of America
John Knox Press
Atlanta, Georgia 30365

Contents

PHILEMON

IN MEMORIAM
FRATRIS MEI CARISSIMI

Beati mortui, qui in Domino moriuntur. Amodo iam dicit Spiritus, ut requiescant a laboribus suis: opera enim illorum sequuntur illos.

1 & 2 THESSALONIANS

Introduction: Getting Clued In

Paul and his companions, Silas and Timothy, wrote these letters to a small, lively, and harassed Christian society which they had established some six to eight months earlier in the metropolis of Thessalonica (modern Salonika) in Macedonia. On the reasonable supposition that these letters were written in Corinth, we can fix their date quite precisely in the spring or early summer of AD 50, composed within a period of five to seven weeks.

They are addressed to an inner city congregation of working-class people meeting in the house of one of its members, a Jewish convert named Jason (Acts 17:5–9). Most of the group were Gentiles, Macedonian Greeks, but there is evidence of a Jewish-Christian minority. This densely populated commercial city, the chief Roman administrative center for northern Greece, had formerly set the tone of the life-style, values, religious interests and outlook on life of these new-born Christians. Now they faced a new situation as believers.

Forced to leave the city because of intense Jewish hostility, the apostle had been waiting anxiously in Corinth for some word about their welfare. Timothy had gone back from Athens at Paul's request to see what he could do for them (1 Thess 3:2). Silas may have stayed close by in the neighboring city of

Beroea. Now the three had made rendezvous in Corinth, the Roman capital of Achaia, where Paul was now working. Timothy had just returned bringing encouraging reports and perhaps a letter from the church in the north (see the hints in 1 Thess 2:13; 4:9, 13; 5:1). Paul responded promptly expressing relief and gratitude while addressing several questions raised by his friends as well as diagnosing some growing pains noticed by Timothy. Within several weeks a messenger returned carrying greetings and another letter from the leaders of the new congregation (perhaps reflected in 2 Thess 1:3, 11; 3:1–5). It was clear to Paul, however, that some of his counsel was being misunderstood either innocently or deliberately, and as their pastoral guide and teacher he proceeded to set them straight. In a rather stiff and formal style this second letter carried his rebuke of their misrepresentation of his apocalyptic teaching. He was further disturbed by their temporizing with some intransigent persons who refused to carry their share of the daily work, probably a consequence of distorted views of spiritual perfectionism (2 Thess 3:6–13).

There continues to be some question among scholars about the origin of this correspondence, the relation of each letter to the other, whether the recipients represent a single or several congregations, how many letters are embodied in the canonical form, and whether, indeed, the so-called second letter is to be assigned to Paul at all or to a later pastor writing in Paul's name. But these are more pedantic concerns. For our purposes it is enough to assign them both to the apostle, written essentially as the canonical tradition has given them to us, and dating from the earliest period of Paul's missionary correspondence with the churches he has organized.

From the standpoint of the preacher and the modern reader it is far more important to assess the issues and concerns reflected in the letters and to note the responses of the writers and also the way in which they deal with the problems. Paul's understanding of the gospel and human inter-relationships is surely indicated not only in what he says but equally in the manner and the attitude in which it is said. We are after both his theological instruction and his leadership style with church people in fair and trying circumstances. To do so we must not only stand with the writer but also identify ourselves with the audience in their enthusiasm for, but innocence about, all that is part of the New Life. Recalling that the letters were probably directed immediately to the leaders of the church to be shared with the whole congregation at worship, we need to distinguish both the larger group and the local leaders who were accountable to the congregation and to the absent apostle. Ministers can certainly identify with them.

The strongly eschatological character of Paul's preaching at Salonika had evoked among these believers a heady enthusiasm about the imminent glory soon to be theirs, hedged also by some uncertainty about their own worthiness and an anxiety about others who were taken prematurely by death. If they were living now in the messianic era, as Paul preached, it surely was occasion for joy and celebration, a Glory Hallelujah! event. But then why were they, as God's chosen, suffering insult, ridicule, and oppression from their neighbors? A few, in the assurance that the climactic final events had already begun, abandoned the normal routine of everyday activity. They wanted to enjoy to the full their new liberation, even though others were becoming annoyed and indignant by their irresponsible and disorderly behavior. Praise-the-Lord converts in their own eyes; shiftless nuisances in the eyes of others.

Some members in the society seemed to have felt that the blessed assurance of their salvation granted them a new openness in relationships with others. Were they actually advocating open marriages as compatible with the new freedom in Christ (1 Thess 4:3–8)? Was there a charismatic element in the congregation which prompted Paul to remind them of the responsibilities as well as the exhilaration of Spirit-empowerment (1 Thess 4:8; 5:19–21)? It may well be. Over against these enthusiasts were members who were uneasy about their own salvation, not yet confident that the complete blessing was theirs (see the "faint-hearted," 1 Thess 5:14). Others worried that the death of loved ones deprived them of their rightful place in the reunion with the coming Lord (1 Thess 4:13–18).

To these we can add questions raised by the local pastor-parish relations committee about the suitability of Paul's leadership and the competence of those whom he left in charge after his hasty exit. All in all their joy in the new life was clouded with confusions, uncertainties, and divergent be-

havior which required a crisis intervention, in the judgment
of the mission team. Like most of us serving congregations,
Paul & Co. had their hands full. A careful reading of his advice
to them will help profile still more sharply the needs of their
community and the way in which the apostle saw fit to inter-
vene. At many points his observations on the gospel of salvation which he is called to preach and his counsels on choices
within everyday discipleship can be brought to bear upon related problems of our churches today. In a way it's one
preacher sharing his faith and experience with others across
the centuries.

A Church on the Go and a Pastor on the Run
(1 Thessalonians 1:1–3:13)

Greetings and Salutations (1:1)

Our form of letter writing hides the identity of the sender until the closing lines. Not so the ancient letter. Paul uses the traditional opening formula in the east: the senders, Paul, Silas, and Timothy; the receivers, the church of the Thessalonians; the greeting, grace and peace. No turning of the pages to see who it's from! Right away we realize that this is not *our* letter, intended for our eyes. With Linus we can say to Charlie Brown: "It makes me feel a little guilty. . . .I always feel like I'm reading someone else's mail!"

We do, that is, until we recognize that it is addressed not to an individual but to a church, a meeting of ordinary people who believe themselves to be called together by God for extraordinary tasks. But we belong to that company too. So we're *not* reading over someone else's shoulder. Paul is speaking to the church wherever and whenever it comes together as God's people in Christ. When the Bible is read, as it often is, from the standpoint of an observer, the word seldom speaks as the Word. Only as we become participants, people who are being addressed directly, is it possible to hear what is being said. You and I and the congregations we serve are addressed by these missionary workers, not just the Christian folk of ancient Salonika. This is our letter too.

As one begins a series of sermons on a group of Paul's letters it would be well to have an introductory sermon on "Listening to the Letters of Paul." We begin as observers visiting a first century congregation, looking and listening. Before long we become participants in common experiences. Finally we let these persons speak *to us,* their words probing our lives, analyzing *our* church life. And we recognize that through their voices it is none other than God calling us to

account, granting us pardon, leading us into new
responsibilities.

The greeting "grace and peace" already sounds like a liturgical formula but, if so, Paul is the first known to use it. Probably he is following a rabbinic practice of associating *shalom*
with such rich words as righteousness, joy, mercy (see "Mercy
and Peace be with you" in the letter of 2 Baruch 78: 2). But for
Paul the conventional religious language is now recast in
meaning because of God's act in Christ. Grace, echoing a common Greek greeting, has come to life for him as the amazing
gift God has given in Jesus Christ. Peace, the most common
term in Judaism for greetings and farewells, has become nothing less than the power of God in Christ to protect, to save, and
to bless his people.

These words are not primarily adjectives but verbs in
character and function. They do not refer to the divine disposition as much as to the divine deeds in human history.
When you've said "grace and peace" you've given expression
to what the NT means by the total condition of salvation.
With recurrent use the greeting would become a convention
like "Grace 'n' peace" comparable to our "Good-bye" (God
be with ye) or "Hello" (Ho, there)—but for these early Christians the simple salutation, not yet worn threadbare, carried
an assurance that God is with us and for us. Retire these
wornout words from the vocabulary of twentieth century
Christians? Not at all! What we need rather is a verbal ar-
chaeology that rescues these artifacts of the past, strips off
the accumulated grime, and puts them back into the working vocabulary of faith!

P.S. Note that in this earliest of all NT writings Paul links
God as Father-Parent with Christ as Lord, leaving us to understand that this is already established in Christian usage at this
time.

Word studies on "grace" and "peace" could generate individual sermons on each of these rich biblical words. "Saying
Grace" might develop the NT emphasis on grace as God's freely given favor exhibited in Christ. It is seen in God's search for
the lost, his pardon a d reinstatement. Why not a sermon
with a title like "Peace-Saying and Peace-Making"? For Paul,
peace involves reconciliation and blessedness under divine
protection. It is far more than the absence of war or mental
pain.

A Church on the Go (1:2–10)

Letters of Paul's time, both public and private, often included an expression of thankfulness for the welfare of the receiver. For Paul, however, the thanksgiving is usually much more extended and serves to introduce and deal with the vital issues of the letter. Paul Schubert, who gave us valuable new insights into the form and function of the Pauline thanksgivings, observed that the thanksgiving begun in 1:2 really extends for the next 43 verses!

It is characteristic of Paul to commence with an affirmation of those to whom he writes, not as a soft-soaping but as a foundation for what he wants to say to them. If indeed he is often scolding and even nitpicking, this cannot undo his basic confidence in their own worth and integrity as newcomers to the Christian life. It's no cheap "You're O.K.; I'm O.K." but a celebration of their new existence and struggle in the context of which he can deal with their misunderstandings and misadventures, and only then. Apart from that, as we pastors learn, negative criticism is demeaning and destructive. Speaking the truth—but in love—is person-nourishing and community-building.

What follows in v. 3 is arresting. Here is the earliest recorded combination of the three basic Christian virtues: faith, love, and hope. Only they do not appear that way, as though, Stoic-fashion, we were presented with a catalog of virtues to be extolled. Paul is behavior-oriented, action-directed, praxis-persuaded, as over against headtripping argumentation and speculative theologizing. Faith *at work;* love *as a labor;* hope *as a stabilizing force.* So he joyfully affirms these brothers and sisters in Christ who are on the move: faithing, loving, hoping great things. It's certain that these key words are seen not as intellectual constructs but powers in operation in the lives of these believers. So he takes pleasure in faith's work, in love's labor, in hope's constancy in their community life. For that, God be praised.

Over against the traditional reference to this constellation of "virtues," there is opportunity to demonstrate in the pulpit message how Paul treats them not as abstractions but as functions. "Faithing, Loving, Hoping": that's a formula for a people in action.

What that faith, love, and hope look like in concrete action is disclosed in a description of how these folks first responded to the gospel as the true word of God and how they are managing in the face of hardship and distress. "Beloved of God," he names them (1:4; the phrase is repeated in 2 Thess 2:13). It was an intimate name for the faithful in the Jewish tradition (see Deut 33:12; Neh 13:26; Sirach 45:1; Baruch 3:36). Said Rabbi Me'ir (2nd century AD), "He that occupies himself in the study of the Law for its own sake merits many things, and, still more, he is deserving of the whole world. He is called friend, beloved [of God], lover of God, lover of mankind..." (*Aboth* 6.1). Paul is bold to speak of these good friends, Gentiles and Jews, as God's dear ones. These Greek nobodies, lost in the huge city of Salonika, are really somebodies in the eyes of the Almighty.

Is this self-serving flattery? A ridiculous claim that his friends are on that account God's friends? Not for a moment. He is convinced that God has laid his hands on them as on him. They must know that they have been chosen deliberately for the divine blessing (v. 4), called (the Greek word behind "chosen," *ekloge*, is equivalent in meaning to another more common word, *klesis*, "calling") into his service. (On "chosen" see Rom 9:11; 11:5, 7, 28. On "calling" see 2 Thess 1:11; 1 Cor 7:20; Eph 4:1; Rom 9:11; Phil 3:14.) It must be remembered also that the literal meaning of "church," in Greek *ekklesia*, is "a calling out."

Out of a history that has come to reserve "calling" to ordained ministers in the church, we ourselves must be corrected by Paul and other NT writers. In the first and basic instance we are all called to Christian commitment. To become a Christian is to be called by God to a new life lived out of obedient love. To be called is to become Christ's person in the world. Derivatively we are also called by the community to specialized tasks within the community. That points to the need for a clarification through preaching of what Christian calling is all about.

The preacher can point up the larger meanings of "Called To Ministry," devoid of the later limitation to ordained ministry. This is a calling directed to each and every member of the congregation to be saved and to serve.

"We know that he has chosen you" (v. 4). Their calling was not imaginary. It could be demonstrated in at least two ways: the reality of the Spirit present (1) in the missionaries' preaching of the gospel in their midst (v. 5), and (2) in the ready welcome these people gave to it (vv. 6–10). Let us examine the evidence more closely.

(1) The preaching of the good news of God's grace for their salvation is not explained by Paul as a sharing of helpful theological information, but the operation of a redeeming power to those who believe it (see Rom 1:16). It is the very dynamite (*dunamis*) of God let loose in an explosive way, blasting away old life patterns and self-defenses to make way for the entrance of the Lord into our lives. Straightforward claims and indirect clues in this letter furnish us with evidence of what Paul understood to be the message of the gospel of salvation. It included:

> Faith in the living and true God, 1:9
> A life of moral integrity, 2:12; 4:1–12
> The expectation of judgment and reunion, 1:10
> God's choice and calling to a new vocation, 1:4
> Christ's death as the salvation event, 5:9
> Life in and through the Spirit, 5:19–22

The fact that the message was preached in the power of the Spirit certified that they are chosen by God, he argues.

(2) Proof of their calling is also found in the faithful hearing that resulted in their own empowerment as a people. The Spirit surely was present in the hearing as it was in the preaching. Just as the missionaries find an inward joy in their work despite hardship and persecution, these Salonika Christians responded affirmatively, experienced the power of the Spirit, and now find joy even in a problematic situation. "Sufferings," an old Jewish saying had it, "are precious because they obtain the Law, the land, and the world to come" (Mekilta on Exod 20:23). The paradox of joy in suffering is a common theme in the NT. That kind of strange happiness that accompanies faithful witness in the face of threat and terror is one of the great signs of God's choice that the martyr churches of the twentieth century have to make to their brothers and sisters in the west. A sermon on "Credentials for Ministry" might raise the question, How can we be sure that we are called? The answer: where the gospel is preached with power, where it is heard not as a human word but the divine word—there is the verification. That can't be dismissed as an illusion. That has the stamp of authority.

"In Macedonia and in Achaia" (v. 7). Indeed the word was getting around among fellow Christians in the area that Salonika had a church that was really on the go. Not only in their home city but all over Greece the news of this remarkable Christian group was spreading. Reports kept coming to Paul in Corinth. Their robust faith had been noised about throughout Greece, yes everywhere.

"Everywhere" was even farther than Paul imagined. For the word got around from Greece to Rome; it moved up into Europe; out from there to the Massachusetts Bay Colony, to Chicago and San Francisco, Rhodesia and India, on and on. We're all linked to Salonika and Jerusalem and Nazareth. We can rejoice with these early missionaries that the word goes out throughout the world. People do turn from their fake divinities and counterfeit saviors to the true God and the Crucified and Risen Lord. A sermon on "How the Word Gets Around" can be developed further by the preacher to sketch the expansion of the church from an obscure Jewish sect to a universal movement of formidable strength and influence. That story continues to get told to the nations through spoken witness and life example.

We may detect in vv. 9–10 a mini-form of the gospel message outlined above. The Good News included:

(1) A vigorous faith in the one true God vs. the fake divinities of human invention (v. 9)
(2) The certainty of Christ's final victory (v. 10)
(3) The resurrection of Christ as the first stage of that victory (v. 10)
(4) Christ the liberator (v. 10)

Defending a Ministerial Style (2:1–12)

Paul is embarrassingly egotistical at times. We stumble over such phrases as "imitators of us and of the Lord," "join in imitating us," "you have an example in us" (see v. 10). Here now we find him in an elaborate self-defense of his ministry among them, almost certainly a reply to local Jewish critics who have denounced Paul and his friends as propagandists for a perverted Judaism. But he is so convinced of his own authority as an apostle, as one through whom Christ is working, that he is stout in defense of his motives and his methods. Without hesitation he denies indignantly that he, Silas, and Timothy were ever status seekers, anxious to gain personal recognition (vv. 3– 6), or worse yet, to take advantage of them for personal benefit (v. 5). They never tried to throw their weight around because they were accredited apostles (v. 6b). (Alternate translation: "we were never burdensome".) First and last they believed that they were answerable only to God who commissioned them with the gospel, not to those who might give them favorable votes in a popularity contest (v. 4).

At the very least he was ready to face his critics. He knew they were wrong and said so. How does that square with the half-apologetic way we defend the church in our day? What other social institution engages in such merciless self-criticism as church people carry on? The church is the butt of many a joke, the target of many an attack by vested power interests in our society. It is beset from within and from without. Preaching on occasion should defend without being defensive. We can learn from Paul to face our critics not succumb to them. A sermon on "The Church on the Offensive" might remind its people of its charter and its commission in a society that leers and lusts but cannot avert disaster.

Renouncing all these charges, the maligned apostle contrasts what the missionaries actually did. Suddenly we see Paul not as the embattled advocate of his own cause but the man expendable for the cause, devoted to their best interests and the gospel's. He and his colleagues were worker-priests among these people. Refusing to accept their support, determined not to be free-loaders, they earned their own keep while they were there (v. 9). They accepted no ministerial discounts at the local shops nor did they expect special privileges as visiting dignitaries.

The images to signify their ministry are illuminating. As a nurse or foster-mother (the equivalent of the "nanny" in English families) cherishes the children in her care, they were gentle and tender in their dealings with these people (v. 7). The Jerusalem Bible considers the nurse to be the mother in its reading, "Like a mother feeding and looking after her own children, we felt so devoted and protective towards you, and had come to love you so much, that we were eager to hand over to you not only the Good News but our whole lives as well" (vv. 7b– 8). The image shifts next to a paternal figure.

They were like fathers taking responsibility for teaching and guiding their children to maturity (v. 11).

An alternate reading in v. 7a permits the translation "On the contrary we became babies (i.e. rather than acting like officious apostles) among you. . . ." In our gender-sensitive society it is interesting to see how this Christian worker employs both masculine and feminine imagery to interpret himself. Further instances can be found in Gal 4:19 where he compares himself to a woman in childbirth. In Philemon v. 10 he is the father who has sired Onesimus in the faith. Is this really Paul the proud, Paul the overbearing, Paul the male chauvinist talking? It scarcely fits the common stereotype we have of the apostle when we hear him speak of mothering and fathering converts to Christ. But this is the real Paul who is standing up.

We have to be prepared for some more surprises as we listen to him explain his feelings towards these people. "We were ready to share with you not only the gospel of God but also our own selves, because you had become very dear to us" (v. 8). He doesn't mean that he has sold his soul to the congregation who can now treat him as their own property. Paul was never a kept man to anyone save his Lord. What he refers to is a voluntary investment of himself in the lives of his people.

A major fallacy among preachers is the assumption that we will be heard for our much speaking. We become so adept with words that we can carry on conversations when our minds are not even on the matter at hand. It can happen that we continue to talk while we ourselves are no longer present in our words. We may then become simply recorded messages, a "noisy gong or a clanging cymbal" in Paul's vivid imagery. But that is talking, not speaking; that is recitation not communication. The gospel for Paul is not an object, verbally packaged and offered for sale. Genuine preaching is not the sales-pitch oratory of the demagogue, whether politician, advertiser, or evangelist, but a divine power at work in a person who can share not only words but a total self with another.

Preaching that is more denunciatory than compassionate, that consistently scolds or whips may get rid of the preacher's hostilities but exhibits nothing of the deep sharing of self expressed in the text. It invites the question, Why are you so angry? rather than, Do you really care?

What is said here about preaching holds good for all our conversations: they may be mere words or shared lives. Not only a model of ministerial style is under discussion here. The secret of transformative human relationships "in the Lord" is being opened up. That, properly experienced, leads us to open our hearts as well as our mouths and the greatest of these is the heart. "Communication as Shared Lives" might be the theme for a series of pulpit messages our word-saturated culture needs to hear. We criticize our parents for their aloofness and timidity in human relationships, but while we touch each other easily we do not do it deeply. The gospel knows that people can be frightened to let other people into their lives, but it insists that true fellowship cannot exist without it. The profound insight in v. 8 might be phrased in a question-topic "Can We Come In?"

The Church That Takes On Trouble (2:13– 16)

Much trouble comes upon us unsolicited. It barges in suddenly and heavily without waiting to be invited and throws us into confusion. Illness, shortages, job failures—they unload their baggage of woe. Other troubles are the fall-out of our own doing, risks we take for unpopular positions taken, unwelcome words spoken, violations of social expectations. Ecclesial communities face the same mixed bag. An inner-city church refusing to flee to the suburbs may face crucial financial problems. An agonized determination to stand against hidden segregationism in the town ("My dear, I'm not prejudiced, but. . . .") may result in threatening phone calls and budget pinching.

In Salonika, the Gentile Christians were already experiencing snubs and other forms of hostility from their fellow citizens, just as the Jewish-Christian churches in Judea earlier had to face from their countrymen (v. 14). Out of his own experience in Philipi, Salonika, and Beroea, Paul could testify personally to the fanatical antagonism of Jewish opponents. But their reaction, while painful to him, could not deter him from his course because he was fully convinced that he was on the Lord's side. Had the Thessalonians accepted Paul's preaching as just one man's point of view, an angry citizenry would not have been stirred up against them. It was precisely because the words they listened to were really heard for what they

were, God's own message of salvation, that the trouble started
in the first place and hadn't stopped (v. 13). They dared to take
him seriously.

That's how it is with the gospel. As an optional view of
human life and how to live, it offers some interesting possibilities for our life in the world. Nor is this inconsequential. Nevertheless it still is to regard the gospel "as the word of men,"
one man's word against another's. But when that word is really heard, however, it is recognized and accepted as the "word
of God" (v. 13). It is the breaking in of a truth that brings our
present world to an end, creates a new situation so that we see
ourselves in a new way, discern other persons in a different
fashion, and understand that God is our beginning and God
our end. That might be the structure of a sermon on "Letting
the Word Go to Work."

What is this word? For Paul it is the event of redemption,
enacted in Christ, and made effectual for others through
preaching. To early believers the word was first and foremost
Jesus Christ the self-disclosure of God in their midst. Second-
ly, it was the message of salvation proclaimed through
preaching. Subsequently that word of God became known also as the book we call the Bible. Strange, then, that so many
Christians reverse the order and make the latter sense the primary sense. Why? Is it because a book may somehow be more
manageable than an event? Are we more comfortable with ob-
jects to handle than with persons, than with the Person, who
cannot be managed or manipulated? Those three meanings of
the word might become the outline of a message on "Encoun-
tering the Word of God."

The Thessalonians were in trouble, deep trouble, with
their fellow citizens. But they had chosen to take on that trouble at the risk to be run when they first heard the word and
agreed to let it order their lives (v. 14). Let the chips fall where
they might. When the church is the church it is inevitably in
trouble because it's bound to be a trouble-maker, a ferment, a
disrupter to high places and sometimes to low. The outcome
of the hearing and doing of the gospel is more likely to be
name-calling than hand-clapping. Was the early church
thinking of times like these when it remembered Jesus' words,
"Happy are you when men insult you and mistreat you and
tell all kinds of lies against you because you are my followers.

Rejoice and be glad, because a great reward is kept for you in heaven" (Matt 5:11– 12,TEV)? The promise of Jesus to his followers is not popularity but persecution. We expect rose gardens and get thorny paths. But we still tie discipleship to success and social recognition and then are disappointed when it doesn't happen. A sermon on "How Not to Win Popularity Contests" might open up the risks as well as the joys of faithful following of the Lord.

The Best Plans Don't Always Work Out (2:17– 20)

In the face of criticism that Paul was either afraid to return to see his friends or had lost interest in them, he lodged a vigorous protest. Some situation, left unstated, had prevented him from doing what he dearly wanted to do: come back and see them (vv. 17– 18). Whatever it was that interfered, he interpreted to be a dark force that continued to frustrate his best laid plans (v.18b). It was certainly not his choice, nor, he believed, God's either. No sooner had he and his new friends been separated (literally, "orphaned") than they found themselves longing for a reunion (v.17).

The child's lament, "You don't love me any more," is translated on the adult level into many different forms of self-pity. In the church it may take the familiar form "The pastor ignores me; he (or she) never calls." "I'm always being confused with someone else." "It's as though we were meeting for the first time." "Why is he (or she) away so much? What we need is someone who isn't forever attending committee meetings or accepting guest preaching invitations but stays home and sticks to business."

Granted a legitimate element in the complaint at times, we know that it can be a petulant appeal for attention and recognition. Instead of a reprimand for a childish attitude, this missionary-pastor offers the reassurance of his love and happiness in them (v. 20). What is his ground of hope and reason for joy in his anticipated appearance before the Lord? These good people whom he has fathered and nursed in the faith. They and they alone are his pride and joy. Strangely enough he never mentions any achievements in renovating the parish house, getting all the commissions to function properly, or boosting the membership. He knows the deeper satisfaction experienced by sensitive pastors and teachers as guides to

change and growth: a boy who begins to do some value sort-
ing; an estranged couple reconciled; single parents learning
new ways of parenting; an older person rescued from the
darkness of depression. Paul won't let the measure of his love
for these people be taken by the number of personal visits he is
able to make. But there are unbreakable ties that bind them
together, a love that bridges every separation.

Is there any more painful ache than separation from loved
ones? The pastor-preacher has to face this human problem
posed by runaway teens, job reassignment, truant spouses,
the finality of death. In this simple passage Paul gives us some
ways of helping the lonely to hold on with a love that will not
let them go. "A Love That Will Not Let Go" can handle both
separations and reunions.

A Cause for Celebration (3:1– 10)

"I could bear it no longer" (v. 5). Deeply concerned to know
how things were going for the church in Salonika, Paul had
sent his associate Timothy in his place to visit and bring a report. There is some uncertainty in the manuscripts about the
designation of Timothy. He is called not only a "brother" but
also "fellow-worker," "minister," and "minister and fellow-
worker" (v. 2).

But there is good reason to qualify both of those titles with
the divine name, so as to read "God's minister" or "God's co-
worker" in the gospel of Christ. I think preference should be
given to the latter (NEB, TEV, JB) rather than the former
(RSV; see 1 Cor 3:9: "God's fellow-workers," NEB). Timothy
is not simply "our co-worker" but "God's co-worker," a remarkable statement of shared ministry. Fellow-sufferers with
Christ and co-workers with God. That's a high estimate of the
nature of ministry, but there is precedent for it in the saying of
Jesus to his disciples: "He who receives you receives me, and
he who receives me receives him who sent me" (Matt 10:40;
see Mark 9:37; Luke 10:16; John 13:20). In the fashion of the
Jewish *shaliach* or "messenger" who goes to another in the
name and under the authority of a rabbi, these persons were
divinely commissioned emissaries.

The Christian as minister or as lay person is not a lackey of
the congregation, nor, for that matter, an errand boy of the Almighty. He or she bears the dignity of one who is an associate

or accomplice with God in the work of the gospel. Think of how that high concept of ministry can correct a self-depreciating understanding, on the one hand, and an incipient messianism, on the other. In a time of secularization of the concept and the practice of ministry we need to hear again our Lord's commission to serve in his name and the apostle's estimate of his role as God's helper. Ours is always the role of an associate in ministry to the Chief Worker. Both ordained and lay ministers are invited to become "Partners in Ministry", a proper title for a sermon.

So Timothy had been working with the struggling congregation in Salonika to help them hold steady in a vulnerable and dangerous situation. Some of them were evidently perplexed by this social conflict they were provoking. The missionary pastors reminded them, in effect, that they never promised them peace and plenty (vv. 3–4). The gospel's safety and security are not convertible into life insurance programs, at least not what is commonly meant by life insurance. There are still aches and pains, risks and troubles in salvation, despite the get-rich-quick solutions promised by the hucksters.

Timothy was back from Salonika. And he brought good news, literally, for the Greek word here is "evangel" (v.6). "He has evangelized us of your faith and love." That's the only secular use of the verb "to evangelize" in the NT, by the way, a striking description of what Timothy had to tell them. What a witness made by a faithful but harassed congregation to an absent pastor: an evangel of their faith and love.

In relief and gratitude Paul shared with them his happiness that they were making a resolute stand in a menacing environment. Further, they haven't bought into the critics' derogation of Paul's purposes. He told them he had taken on a new lease on life because of them. "We live if you live secure in the Lord" (v. 8). That can be seen as the Christian revision of the theme of transactional analysis: from "I'm O.K.; you're O.K.," essentially self-regarding, to "You're O.K.; then I'm O.K.," essentially life for and from others. It's important enough to be developed sermonically.

Paul looks forward anxiously to a visit with them, eager to assist them in their own developing faith, mindful too of the new life and cheer they have brought to him (vv. 9–10). Notice how Paul understands ministry as a mutual act between pas-

tor and people. It is a giving and receiving on both sides, a
ministering and a being ministered to. What comfort and joy
they have given him (vv. 7, 9); what new strength he wants to
give them (v. 10).

Some clergy have yet to learn this. Their view of ministry
requires the leader to be the answer-person, the inexhaustible
resource, the primary decision-maker. If it is true that a generous but misguided laity tends to beatify their pastors, it is a
sober fact that the self-understanding of the clergy often validates the idolatry. Such pretentious omnicompetence is not
only ridiculous; it violates the meaning of ministry which the
NT presents as a mutuality of service in the name of the Lord.
Blessed it is to give. Blessed too, and often more difficult, it is
to receive. We ask ourselves: How are we permitting the congregation to act as God's helper to us in ways other than a
Christmas bonus? "Pastor and People in Mutual Ministry" is
not so suitable as a title, but it profiles a sermon theme that
can enrich our common understandings of ministry.

A Prayer for Love in the Church (3:11–13)

With full heart the missionary pastors conclude with a
prayer to the Father God and the Lord Jesus that their long-
ings for a reunion may be realized. We note that, in what may
be the earliest recorded Pauline prayer, the person of Jesus the
Messiah (Christ) and Lord is joined with the Father God (the
most common name for God in the Synoptic Gospels; see 2
Thess 1:1). This is the heart and center of Pauline Christology.
Jesus, Messiah and Lord, is the very self-manifestation of God.
Ditheism would be unthinkable for a former Pharisaic Jew.
No more would Jewish Wisdom theology think of God and
Wisdom as separable deities. Paul's language is liturgical and
confessional not philosophical or theological. With the *Shema*
(see Deut 6:4) he would affirm the oneness of God who is finally all in all (1 Cor 15:28) and who has acted for human salva-
tion in the person of Jesus.

It is sound Pauline theology that finds expression in the
Ephesian declaration: "Before the world was made, God had
already chosen us to be his in Christ, so that we would be holy
and without fault before him" (Eph 1:4, TEV). If doctrinal
preaching (rare enough these days) concentrates solely on
questions of *being* in the relationship of Christ to God, it will

continue to pose problems both for preachers and people. But if, with Paul, Christological preaching centers on the *activity* of God as he makes himself knowable and his purposes understandable in the Son, then doctrinal preaching can take on fresh meaning today.

The prayer is that love for one another may abound and increase. John's Gospel reformulates the Synoptic saying of Jesus about the two-fold law—love to God; love to neighbor—into a new commandment, "Love one another as I have loved you." This becomes the hallmark of true discipleship (John 13:35). The apostle is echoing this deeply imprinted tradition of the early church. With John and other NT writers, however, the self-understanding of the church leads unhappily to drawing the boundaries of shared love about the faithful chiefly and perhaps only. Significantly enough Paul avoids any such restrictions by adding "and *to everyone else*" (v. 12; "the whole human race," JB; and note the same universality in 5:15 and Gal 6:10).

Imposing restrictions upon the love object gets dangerously close to loving ourselves by loving our kind, in this case our fellow-Christians. But it is clear that the historical Jesus showed his radicalism just at this point. Nothing other than the inclusive love of God which embraces the entirety of humanity is the model for those who would be his true children (see Luke 6:32–36, etc.). That means an unconditional, unqualified reaching out to everyone in the human family, foreign refugee and next door neighbor alike. In Paul's crisp putting of it: "To one another and to everyone, as much as we to you" (v. 12). They are to love one another and everyone else just as Paul loves them.

So Christ the Lord challenges them and us to love without limitation and thus make them and us to be numbered among his people at his coming (v. 13). The converse would be equally true. Only those who can be stirred to this kind of loving are fit to be part of his company in the presence of God. "Love Is Never Blind." Love sees more, not less. Real Christians make great lovers! There are deep insights in this simple prayer for preaching on the ranges of love.

Two Issues: Christian Life-Style and Life After Life
(1 Thessalonians 4:1–5:28)

Christian Sexuality (4:1–8)

Paul as a good Jew conceives religious faith not as a concept but as practice. It finds expression in how one conducts oneself. It is behavioral and operational, a response of the total person. His very language in discussing the marks of a Christian life-style shows the traditional Jewish insistence upon orthopraxis (right conduct) rather than on orthodoxy (right doctrine) which the Greek philosophical influence in Christianity was to require. In the present passage the literal rendition of his words is "You received from us *how you ought to walk* and to please God" (v. 1). Discipleship was a way of walking or acting, a *halakah* in his ancestral language. He would make no distinction, as we do, between theoretical and applied ethics. The Christian life is described as peripatetic (Greek, *peripatein*): "itinerant, always on the march."

So at this point the pastor-counselor wishes to remind his Salonika friends of some instructions, previously given and now restated for some good reason (perhaps in response to a report or a letter), on how to practice a discipleship life-style. Nor are these friendly tips on how to get the most out of life, growing out of his own experiences. They are dominical directions; they carry the authority of the indwelling Christ. The context makes it clear that Paul is restating and adapting the common tradition of the early church which was believed and behaved as the word of the Risen Lord who is the Speaker and Transmitter of these disciple traditions in the church. "For you know what instructions we gave you through the Lord Jesus" (v. 2; see "in the name of the Lord Jesus," NEB, "o the authority of the Lord Jesus," JB).

The basic mandate is: They must be separated from whatever defiles and degrades and be wholly devoted to God in body and soul; this is God's will for them. Hence they are to abstain from all forms of sexual immorality (v. 3). The theme is a recurrent one in the Pauline correspondence and undoubtedly points up the clash between Jewish Christian sexual ethics and the ethics prevailing in Roman society of the time. Whether *skeuos* in v. 4 is to be translated as "wife" or "body" is a fine point that does not alter materially the main thrust. However it is a difficult passage as a glance at several translations of the Greek text will attest. One may read it as an admonition to respect one's wife and to hold her in holiness and honor by abstaining from fornication. Then the reference to not wronging the brother (v. 6) may refer to adultery, or, alternatively, not encouraging anyone to promiscuity. Apropos the latter is the possibility that some members in the church have defended a continuation of their former sexual conduct on the basis that they have already been saved; hence life in the body is secondary and inconsequential (the "weak" of 5:14?).

Or perhaps the wrong done to one's brother may refer to lawsuits or business practices: "defraud his brother in business" (RSV Margin). This is to be avoided. Still another possibility is to read *skeuos* in the sense of one's own body, in which case the sense may be expressed with the NEB "Each one of you must learn to gain mastery *over his own body*, to hallow and honour it." So then these may be counsels to the married, to those who are entering marriage, to both the married and the businessman.

Whatever the references, and we understand the apostle to speak of marriage and adultery, it is clear enough that God's call is to purity and holiness of life (v. 7), validated by the solemn claim "whoever disregards this, disregards not man but God, who gives his Holy Spirit to you" (v. 8). Every form of uncleanness is to be firmly renounced.

It is, of course, an extremism to put the church and the world into an antithetic relationship and to deny the latter in the fashion of the world-renouncing medieval equation, "the world, the flesh, and the devil." On the other hand early Christianity was not about to take its agenda, its direction, or its standard of values *from* the world. To do so for Paul meant life according to the flesh where the secular standards prevailed.

What is to be said about our own society with its acceptance of premarital sex, trial and short term cohabitation; open marriages; and its toleration of variant sexual orientations? More to the point, how do we respond to church people who favor accommodation to alternate life-styles, relaxing any possible tensions between the NT conception of *hagiasmos*, consecration, and privatistic freedom? Are we in a fair way to reinstating the old Greek maxim, "Man is the measure of all things"? Are we converting heteronomy, accountability to a moral law more basic than social custom, to a form of autonomy, answering to only those obligations which the individual determines? The outcome is an increasing anarchy that is destructive of community and society. Paul steadfastly believes that there is an unbridgeable difference between faith (holy living) and worldliness (degenerate secularism) but we want it both ways. A sermon entitled "Is the Church a Mirror of Society?" should raise the question for pastor and people whether the church is simply to accept and sanctify prevailing social norms (the "American Way"), or derive its own standards from the gospel, quite apart from where the total society is at.

Why not address the issue of the theology of marriage? Sociologists, marriage counselors, novelists, and TV writers all assume their right to criticize and/or ridicule marriage and the family. Biblical preaching surely must interpret anew for this Me-generation the meaning of Christian marriage. The biblical convictions about life-long covenant relationships and enduring commitments must encounter a people who fear both because they fear community and seek security in shifting allegiances. The church ought to be at least as persuasive as Olympic skating coach Gus Lussi who can describe commitment to championship as an all-absorbing, all-demanding dedication. "Covenant as Life Tenure" is a sermon title which points to the issue. "Call to Consecration" says it another way where consecration is not confused with pietism but identified with a pattern of life shaped by the gospel.

The Loving Community (4:9–12)

Commendations had previously been given on the high quality of caring relationships which marked this Christian community in Macedonia (1:3; 3:6, 12). Yet another reference is made to it and in a form that suggests that the Thessalonians had written for guidance on this matter. Specific questions may be referred to in 4:9 and 13. The closely related admonitions set out in vv. 11–12 suggest that the leaders may

have asked about how to deal with some whose high enthusiasm about their new life and the expected coming of the Lord
was creating some problems for the total group. It was an internal situation in the church; hence "love one another" (v.
9b) here clearly refers to the Christian brother and sister (v.
9a).

For Paul and for the early Christian communities, the central reality in Jesus' teaching, remembered and made deter-
minative for their life together, was the inclusive love of God,
enacted in the words and works of Jesus. It was indeed the
heart and the fulfilment of the historic Mosaic law (Rom
13:8–10). He insisted that the missionary preachers and
teachers were the story tellers of that love of God which was
demonstrated in Christ. Thus he can say, "You yourselves
have been taught by God to love one another" (v. 9b). God is
the Master Teacher; the apostles were only student teachers.
The only way to extend brotherly/sisterly love in Christian
terms is to experience it in God's act of love for humankind in
Jesus Christ, and let it express itself intensely in relationships
with others. He wants his Thessalonian friends to be more and
more love-possessed, love-directed.

It is interesting and helpful to us as leaders in the Christian
community today to watch for evidences in the letters for
Paul's missionary strategy in human relationships. We have
noticed from the outset of this letter how the pastor can stir
his readers to new action without making them feel that they
have failed miserably up to this point. "We are strengthened
by your faith (3:7); we want to help you find what is now lack-
ing in your faith (3:10). We thank God for your love in action;
you do hold in loving concern not only the members of your
own little group, but all the people of Christ throughout the
province of Macedonia (v. 10a). Only understand that the possibilities of love are unlimited; let your love increase and
abound to everyone (v. 10b). You must never set boundaries
on learning to love." So we might paraphrase what we read in
these sections.

The preacher is presented here with one of many reminders in the NT that the love of God can never be truly experienced except it leads to a loving concern for other persons.
To love God is to love the brother and the sister in ever-widen-
ing circles of inclusion. One might let a sermon develop out of
three texts set in interaction; the passage in Rom 13:8–10;

these verses in 1 Thess 4:9–10a; and the paean in praise of love in 1 Cor 13.

Vv. 10b–12. In Salonika that meant specifically that the enthusiasm and excitement generated by their new life together must not be allowed to disrupt the community by any negligence in doing their daily work. Nor should they become tattlers and busy-bodies, dabbling in other people's affairs. This is the first hint in the letter of a community problem which will engage Paul's attention more than once. Some may have claimed this right to community support as persons who felt specially endowed with the gifts of the Spirit (5:19–22 may provide a clue). Whatever else, such persons were proving to be nuisances and troublemakers. The problem already was serious enough to call for further consideration in the exchange of letters, as we know (see 2 Thess 3:6–15). Drones and free-loaders had no place in Paul's concept of community which called for shared work (Gal 6:2) by everyone in the context of personal responsibility and activity (Gal 6:5). Epicurus had taught his fellow-seekers after the good life "Live quietly (*lathe biosas*)," but Paul's similar counsel is set in correlation with "earn your own living." Quiet down; cool it, he counsels these disturbers of the peace; attend to your own duties; take responsibility for yourself (see v. 12b "Be dependent on nobody")—just as we have always urged.

Did experiencing the intimacy and joy of the new community often lead some to excess till they became drags and disturbances to the others? Modern young people who have experienced something of the fulfilment and frustration of "life together" in the commune movement would easily understand these counsels from a first century writer. Nor is it beyond the comprehension of most congregations and pastors who know how rapidly rights and privileges are claimed in the group before responsibilities and work are accepted. The basic dynamics of social organization and social disruption can be read between the lines of this ancient letter.

One could find some pertinent advice in this passage for a message on "From Observer To Participant," a reflection on group dynamics and community building. Three staccato commands: Keep calm! Attend to your own business! Work! There may be other things that should be added but these three, put to action, could certainly draw anyone from the role of a curious bystander to that of a contributing participant in the work of the church. We ought not be fooled by their simplicity.

The appeal to full involvement in all the affairs of community life is defended in v. 12 by two practical purposes: (1) that they bring no discredit on the church from outsiders (v. 12a); (2) that they not become parasites (v. 12b). Paul does not regard the church as an enclave but a component of the larger society. It has its own values and standards, to be sure, but it is not an end in itself. It is freed from the domination of the world, but it accepts responsibility for that world. Alone among the NT letter writers, he insists that one of the measures of Christian action is the effect it has upon the larger world. Note also 1 Cor 14:16, 23– 24 where he deals with another form of the problem of spiritual gifts and its repercussion beyond the church into the larger community. It really matters to Paul what the unbeliever thinks about the church!

The fellowship we know as church exists not for self-indulgence and private happiness but to address the world, to expose its injustice, to offer forgiveness, to make the unbelieving world part of the new community in Christ. The idlers in the church at Salonika and the troublemakers in the church through history are indicted because they impede the social witness of the church. That is a far more serious accusation than that they are annoying the brotherhood. It reminds us of John's appeal through Christ for the unity of the church in relationship to mission: "so that the world may believe" (Jn 17:21, 23).

That's a remarkable new criterion by which to test the church and its ministry: the effect on the outsider. Add that to the other two: (1) Jesus proclaimed as Lord, and (2) the church strengthened, and we have three Pauline tests of the true church, themes for a sermon or sermon series on "Real and Counterfeit Churches".

Death and the Day of the Lord (4:13– 18)

Death and dying were no less problems for ancient than modern people. Philosophers could argue the indestructability of the human soul, but for many death was believed and feared to be "one unbroken night of sleep" (Aeschylus, *Eumenides* 651) from which there was no awakening. The assurance that the initiate in the Mystery cults would inherit a blessed immortality was one response to the pervasive fear of death (see Heb 2:14, 15). For Salonika Christians, the issue centered in anxiety about the relation of their Christian dead to the final events of the Lord's Coming. Their own expectation of the approaching Great Gittin'-up Morning in which they would share led them to dismay at the passing of friends and loved ones who might not experience that glorious hour.

Paul's counsel at this point is the most detailed description of the Final Advent to be found anywhere in the NT. Nevertheless its borrowed imagery and allusions give us only an impressionist rather than a pictorial view and leave many questions unanswered, perhaps for the Thessalonians, but certainly for later Christians trying to understand the Christian hope. Elements of the statement may be compared with such passages as Matt 24:31 and 1 Cor 15:52, on "the trumpet of God" (v. 16); John 5:25–29 on the call to life by Christ (v. 16b); Dan 7:13 and 2 Enoch 3: 1ff. on the imagery of the clouds that form a heavenly chariot for the returning Lord and his people (v. 17).

Behind the brocade of images, most of them in common with apocalyptic writings of the time, there are some penetrating faith statements by the apostle which are presuppositional to our understanding of his faith. When Paul wants to describe the new condition of existence for those who have come to faith and experience the presence of Christ in their lives, he uses the phrases "in the Lord," "in Christ Jesus," or "in Christ." When he wishes to speak of the prospect of a final and everlasting companionship beyond death, as he does here, he uses the phrase "with Christ" (see Phil 1:23; 2 Cor 13:4). Not only in this mortal life but beyond it, the believers will be inseparably related to the one who is the Lord of the living and of the dead. As in life, so also in death they belong to Christ (Rom 14:8; 1 Thess 5:10). In the final reunion at the End they constitute his company in attendance (v. 14; see 1 Cor 15:23). Together with the living, the reunited company "will always be with the Lord" (v. 17). There is no Lord without his people. There are no people apart from their Lord. It is a corporate hope, not individualistic; Christocentric, not egocentric.

Alternatively, it may be noted that the phrases "through

Jesus" or "in Jesus" in vv. 14 and 16 may be read instrumen-
tally where the emphasis is thrown not on the sphere of existence but rather on the agency of Christ in the awakening of
those now sleeping. It is through him that God brings the dead
to the new Day (v. 14). It is through him that God effects the
resurrection of the dead (v. 16).

On either reading Paul gives no account here of an inter-
mediate state between private death and the public event of
the Parousia except to assert that all are somehow within his
care. There is nothing, not even death, "the last enemy," that
can "separate us from the love of God in Christ Jesus our
Lord" (Rom 8:39). That is the final word in an eschatology
which is unshakeable in its conviction that God through
Christ is the destroyer of death in all its myriad forms and the
giver of life. That is another voice than Apollo's in *The Eumenides* of Aeschylus: "The life once lost can live no more. For
death my father (Zeus) has ordained no healing spell; all other
 hings his effortless and sovereign power casts down or raises
up at will" (651).

But the word of Christian hope is: Not so! We belong to the
Lord forever! And that firm hope for Paul is established on the
authority of the Lord Himself. What is the blessed assurance?
"Jesus is mine"? Rather, We are *his!* For the Christian God is
the eternal refuge and strength against every foe. Whether in
life or in death, in our precarious present and in our unknown
future, we are sustained in the knowledge that God "never, no,
never, no, never" forsakes his own.

There may be many details in this passage that carry little
meaning to modern Christians. Angelic trumpet calls, spacial
descents and ascents presuppose another view of the universe
than we accept. But what stands at the center remains the assurance of hope: God overcomes death with life, and offers a
friendship that nothing actual or imaginable can destroy.
Preaching must clarify the Christian understanding of "Life
After Life" to rescue it from the popular guarantees of immortality. The clue to what life "with the Lord" will be like must
be read out of the realities of Christian discipleship in this life,
not in ESP and encounters of a third kind, or even the emotional orgies some associate with the Rapture.

"Love Is Stronger Than Death" is a theme title that might
let the texts of Rom 8:37–39 and 1 Thess 4:13–18 speak to

each other and become a common voice of hope to Christians
who continue to live in fear of death.

"Always with the Lord" of v. 17 is explained further by 1
Cor 15:23 "those who belong to Christ" and leads our thought
from the child's question "Who do I belong to?" to the adult
search for identity. A fruitful sermon theme might be: Knowing who we are—we are Christ's people—we belong to him.

Apocalyptic Anxieties and Trust in God (5:1–11)

Evidently the fainthearted in the Salonika congregation
were not only worried about the salvation of their beloved
dead, but also uncertain about their own prospects. Perhaps
they wished they had a secret knowledge about the End Time
that might guarantee they wouldn't lose out themselves. They
didn't want to be taken by surprise and find themselves ex-
cluded from the blessed kingdom. They felt they were entitled
to know God's time table, not just out of human curiosity, but
because they would then get themselves prepared to participate in it (v. 4). The way Paul begins, "as to times and seasons" (v. 1), it appears that the issue had been raised in a letter
from the church.

The apostle reminds them of what they already had been
told: the Day of the Lord comes suddenly, unexpectedly, completely, like a burglar breaking in at night (v. 2). That is to say,
that's how it happens for those oblivious to the true situation.
For them it will be a disruptive advent, destroying their
world, upsetting their normalcy.

We are reminded of the similar emphasis by Jesus who in
parable upon parable warned of the destructive effect of the
Kingdom's incursion into their human situation. Professor
John Dominic Crossan points out that the Parable of the Good
Samaritan had as its original point "the reversal caused by
the advent of the Kingdom in and through the challenge to ut-
ter the unutterable and to admit thereby that other world
which was at that very moment placing their own under radical judgment" (*In Parables*, 1973, p. 66). To which could be
added the Rich Man and Lazarus; the Pharisee and the Publican; the Wedding Guest; the Great Supper; and the Prodigal
Son. All speak of challenge and threat to the existing order.

But those open to God need not be taken by surprise, Paul
urges (v. 4). They are day people, not night people, and they

know what the new day will be like because they have already begun to experience it. The fainthearted, doubting their own worth and God's acceptance, should understand that Christ has clarified beyond all doubt the divine purpose to save, not destroy, those who have given themselves to him. In his own words "For God has not destined us to the terrors of judgement, but to the full attainment of salvation through our Lord Jesus Christ. He died for us so that we, awake or asleep, might live in company with him" (vv. 9– 10, NEB).

The craving to know what the future holds for each of us lies behind all kinds of human probing of the future from electronic forecasting in the business community to the use of astrological charts to find personal happiness. There are many new forms of the age old questions about "times and seasons" which disturbed the Christian community of Salonika who were frightened that they would not be part of the new day.

The apostle's counsel on these apocalyptic anxieties is instructive to Christians in any age. God's Hour is always a surprise to those who least expect it, those who imagine they can manage for themselves quite nicely and refuse to recognize the threats to peace and security in their societies (v. 3). Like the *shalom* prophets of Jeremiah's day, they paper over the cracks in the walls and announce that all is well. God's coming is always disruptive and destructive to these purveyors of good times.

But Paul is concerned about immature Christians who should be living in the light and instead act as though they're still in the dark. Why should the children of God be panicked at the prospect of God's coming in judgment when they are assured that his intention is not to destroy but to save? How can they worry about their own survival in the times of testing if they believe that Jesus Christ offered himself to death that they might live? What else is the gospel hope than that we shall always live with him? For Paul the true believer is not one who nervously assesses his chances for glory in an apocalyptic age, but one who practices the Christian graces of faithing, loving, and hoping (v. 8; see 1:3) in the confidence that God never deserts his own. Resolute action in making new lives for themselves is what was required in view of the imminent eschatological crisis.

Paul doesn't advise them to improve upon their apocalyptic calculations, counting the hours and checking their calendars to pinpoint the time of the day of the Lord. Perhaps he would have smiled at the Curé de Torcy (in G. Bernanos, *The Diary of a Country Priest*): "Surely I may be allowed to snigger at folk who keep bursting into song before God has raised His conductor's baton." Worried about life? Disturbed about death? Afraid you'll not make it? Look, Christ died for us so that whatever comes *we shall live with him* (v. 10). In a later letter to some Christians in Rome, he would say, "Whether we live or die, then, *we belong to the Lord.* For Christ died and rose to life in order to be the Lord of the living and of the dead" (Rom 14:8–9 TEV). The future holds no terror for those who know who is Lord. We indeed do not know *when* he comes, but we do know *who* comes and in that knowledge we stand secure.

Sermon possibilities leap out at us. "How to Live in an Apocalyptic Age." In a troubled and fear-ridden world, the assurance of the text in vv. 9–10 can make the difference between "Panic and Peace." Fainthearted folk may be nervously preoccupied with "Upcoming Events." "Facing God's Future" might develop the theme that the faithful ought to be ready to let God lead them into his future unafraid. Then, as now, there was Christian preaching that served to inflame apocalyptic anxiety. With pastoral care Paul stands with those who try to cool it, offering comfort to the distressed and centering hope on God's purpose of redemption. Paul provides the better way.

Leadership and Spiritual Gifts (5:12–22)

Some final matters remain for attention which affect the life of this community in the capital city. Probably the congregation as a whole is addressed when Paul urges them to hold in respect and love their leaders who manage the practical affairs of the group life, including matters of counsel and discipline. No titles are given for these workers but their functions are alluded to and it is clear that they perform an indispensable, if not always a popular, service to the community. We are not to conclude that we have here a distinct separation between clergy and laity. That develops in later stages of the organizational growth of the church. For Paul ministry is performed by the whole church under the guidance of appointed leaders.

What are their special needs and what does the apostle consider to be marks of an effective church? Even though he is speaking to a very particular situation which had its full share of problems, we can detect a conception of what it means to be the church in all kinds of situations. Leaders are to be recognized and esteemed (vv. 12– 13). Peaceful relationships are to be cherished (v. 13b). (Compare his earlier counsel: "live quietly," 4:11, and see 2 Cor 13:11; Rom 12:18.) The whole church, not simply the leaders, is to deal firmly but with patience with extremists (the idlers, v. 14); to cheer up the apprehensive (the fainthearted, v. 14), and to support the morally weak (v. 14). This is part of what it means for a congregation to be in ministry, not simply receiving ministry from others, the leaders for example, but practicing ministry *to each other*.

The reference to leadership in vv. 12– 13 might become the basis for a sermon on the contributions made by those in varied positions of leadership in the church, so easily accepted, so frequently unrecognized. All the counsels to a loving and helpful ministry, each to the other in the fellowship (vv. 13b– 15), ought to be reflected upon as descriptive of a true congregation in the Lord. These are what it means for pastor and people to be "Called To Ministry."

Vv. 15– 18. Basic to it all is that Jesus-love which refuses to engage in the popular forms of retaliation, tit-for-tat, that a secular society endorses (v. 15). Injustice done; injustice returned. Dirty tricks done; dirty tricks retaliated. Violence suffered; revenge in kind repaid. Instead of that, they are summoned always to do good (that is, to manifest love) to one another. And more, to *everyone*, believer and non-believer (v. 15; see 3:12). God's will for the church is that its people learn to face all that comes with an irrepressible joy (v. 16), a prayerfulness (v. 17), and an unwavering gratitude in all circumstances (v. 18).

That disposition is not a Stoical indifference to outward circumstance, an unruffled endurance with tight upper lip through changing fortunes. For Paul the Christian is vulnerable. He or she can be hurt, disappointed, confused, defeated. But never driven to total despair, never forsaken, never destroyed (2 Cor 4:8– 11). It is the love and power of the indwelling Christ that gives the strength to meet every situation life

presents. Not that every event is a blessing in disguise; hence
we are thankful for it. This is unrealistic, a romantic approach
to life that blurs the distinction between good and evil. The
key to Paul's extraordinary advice—"Whatever happens, give
thanks to God"—is that Christians meet every event knowing
that they are not alone. The Lord of life and death is with
them. That's the source of the constant joy, constant prayer,
the unqualified thanksgiving. So John Wesley on his death
bed could whisper his last words, "The best of all is: God is
with us."

Doing what's best for everyone, rejoicing, praying, thank-
ing (vv. 15b–18): that might outline the major points of a sermon on "Behaving Like Christians." Christians stand between
a world of man's making and a new world of God's making
and ask, What are we to do? We are not to be reduced to helplessness by it, but instead to a benevolent activity in the context of joy, prayer, and gratitude. One might single out the
final, difficult entreaty "Give thanks whatever happens" to reflect through a sermon on how we usually meet prosperity
without remembering to be thankful and adversity with no
need to be thankful. Saying thanks is only one small part of
being thankful. The passage here has a complement in Col
3:17.

Vv. 19–22. With a mind to the extremists who may have
claimed special revelations of the Spirit, and at the same time
addressing the whole community, Paul observes that the authentic gifts of the Spirit are to be cherished (v. 19). Out of his
own experience in the churches and out of the long tradition
of his people he knew that the Spirit could be misinterpreted
and even impersonated. Not every alleged prophet was Spirit-
inspired. Not every utterance was God's voice speaking. Every
valid gift of the Spirit, he believed, was a power of God released for service to others (1 Cor 12:6–7). Elsewhere he
makes clear what is involved in his general counsel here:
"Test everything" (5:21). That includes all spiritual gifts, not
simply prophecy. What are the tests that identify the authentic action of the Spirit? We have distinguished three: (1) Is
Jesus confessed as Lord? (1 Cor 12:3); (2) Is the church built
up? (1 Cor 14:3–5, 12, 26b); (3) Are others led from unbelief to
belief? (1 Cor 14:16, 23–25). Nothing is said here about spiritual thrills and private pleasures in the experiences. Against

every other notion of spiritual gifts for personal benefit Paul insists that a *charisma* is an empowerment to meet the needs of others in the name of Christ the Lord. It must result in what is for the good of others not for harm (vv. 21b–22; see 1 Cor 12:7; 14:12).

The new concern about spiritual gifts in the church today needs that level-headed counsel from a veteran preacher of the gospel and pastor to churches. Charismatic activities are not protected by a special immunity, in Paul's understanding. The Spirit must not be repressed, but neither is it to be obeyed in blind belief. The text here in vv. 19–22 must be read in the larger perspective of the discussion of spiritual gifts in 1 Cor 12-14. Then let sermons develop out of the total discussion on such topics as "The Gifts of the Spirit"; "Empowering the Church Through the Spirit"; "The Spirit Is a We-Experience."

A Prayer for the Church (5:23–24)

Again Paul is moved to prayer for the future salvation of the new community. Brief as it is, it gives expression to his own insights into the gospel. In the earlier prayer, he had spoken of Christ's work in purifying their hearts to be consecrated to God (3:13). He had further explained this consecration as not only devotion to God, but a separation from the world and its ways in disciplined moral living (4:3–8). In this final prayer he emphasizes that the consecration desired is total not partial. It is not a matter of purity of heart only; it must mark the person as a total self ("spirit, soul, and body") and thus lay claim upon both inward purposes and desires and also their behavioral expression. They are to be holy through and hrough. Thus they will be prepared to be among Christ's company at the End.

This is God's will for them (4:3). This is their responsibility (4:1). This is what God will help make possible for them (v. 24). What the church will be, it must now begin to be. That is a demand put upon them. But paradoxically it is also something *given* to them as well as *expected* from them. "God will do it" (v. 24b). God gives what he asks, but only as they actively participate and make it their own, not passively wait for it to happen.

God is called "the God of peace." The model of the new

community is described in Rom 14:17 as "righteousness, peace, and joy in the Holy Spirit." But these have their origin in God. He is a God of peace where peace is understood to be a saving power which protects the congregation from evil, consecrates, and blesses them.

"Take my life and let it be consecrated, Lord, to thee." We have sung it many times. But what precisely is meant by "consecration"? The passages we have been looking at in this letter, 3:13; 4:3–8; 5:23 should open up some new meanings in that well-worn word. It surely belongs in any glossary to be discussed in a series of sermon word studies on "The Meaning of Religious Language" or "The Vocabulary of Faith." "Prayer Is Answered!" might be the topic on which to expound further the apostle's conviction in v. 24 that the prayer for consecration and purity will certainly be answered. He knows that the God who is the Caller is also the Doer and he can be counted on. He is the Enabler without whose assistance the appeals to peace and to moral maturity would be vain.

Farewells and a Blessing (5:25–28)

The pastor who prays continually for his beloved friends in Christ also knows his own need for their prayers (v. 25). They need him, and he needs them. As they pray for themselves and for others, they are reminded of how he, their mother-nurse and their father in Christ, stands in need of their prayerful intercession. Luther's concept of the priesthood of all believers, so commonly misunderstood, embodies the same understanding of the mutuality of ministry in the Christian community. The church at prayer is a church where pastor and people are praying for others, where pastors pray for their people, and where people are praying for their pastors who, like them, are standing in the need of prayer. Beneath the quick words of praise or criticism to which congregations are prone should be the affectionate concern each for the other voiced in prayer. Then both praise and blame can be give and accepted constructively. We can thank God that we are given to each other.

Give my affectionate greetings to everyone in the fellowship, he says, and that must include the troublemakers as well as the leaders (v. 26). And then, with characteristic firmness, adds that he expects everyone to hear and heed what he has written. It suggests some further reflections on "Administering Discipline in Love."

Fare you well. So long, we say. For this man the conventional leavetakings are set aside. From these good friends in Christ he takes his leave with a prayer: May the extravagant goodness of God we experience in Christ be yours (v. 28). That would really be to fare well.

Pushing God's Calendar
(2 Thessalonians 1:1 – 2:17)

Evidently Paul's earlier letter to the Salonika Christians did not have all the affect he desired. Doubts persisted about how they would fare in the final reckoning before the throne of God. Nervous apprehensions increased about the claims of some enthusiastic extremists that the Day long promised was already dawning. And the disruptive behavior of these same radicals in expecting to be supported, despite their refusal to carry their share of daily work, threatened to destroy the peace and order of the community. Learning of the deteriorating condition, Paul addresses the church more specifically and firmly. One more time with gusto! We noted earlier that some interpreters regard the letter to be addressed to another, perhaps a Jewish-Christian group in the Macedonian capital. Others think it was sent to another city, or even written much later by a Pauline church leader, using the first letter as a model.

Learning How to Face Hostility (1:1 – 7a)

It is possible that in the first section of this letter through the prayer which concludes in 2:17 Paul has in mind particularly those he terms the fainthearted.

Vv. 3– 5. Perhaps some of the over anxious members of the society in Salonika were embarrassed and uneasy at what they felt was extravagant and undeserved praise by Paul in his earlier letter to them. They were not the first to find it difficult to accept a compliment! In reply Paul responds that he must affirm them publicly since they continue to face bravely a hostile environment without falling apart (vv. 3– 4). Of course they have problems and he wants to talk about them. But first let them take heart with him that their faith remains steadfast, in fact is growing, their love is increasing, and patient endurance is not faltering but strengthening. You can't seriously doubt yourself when that is happening. In fact the hate and hardship they, and Paul too, are constantly confronting must be understood as humanity's defiant opposition to the kingdom of love. Their faith and endurance is proof of God's judgment that they are worthy to share in that Kingdom (v. 5). Can we hear an echo of Jesus' warning and reassurance: "How blest are those who have suffered persecution for the cause of right; the kingdom of Heaven is theirs" (Matt 5:10 NEB).

Vv. 6–7a. That divine judgment, however, has another side. In a fashion reminiscent of the ancient *lex talionis* Paul anticipates a divine recompense upon those who now afflict the righteous. Rest and relief to you and me, he promises, punishment upon the oppressor. That will be the reversal of fortune that marks the great and terrible Day of the Lord. They know that God must prevail ultimately.

Injury and pain are of many sorts, all equally unsought, but brought on for various reasons and endured for different motives. To be sure Paul can even interpret his personal health problem theologically as a reminder of God's all-sufficiency and his own weakness (2 Cor 12:7–10). But suffering for the Kingdom of God here means mistreatment, ridicule, and abuse at the hands of those who are convinced Christians are a threat to the established order they uphold. Back of the attack is the age-old problem of human perversity displayed in intensified opposition to God's cause in the world, the stubborn resistance to the way of love in human affairs. The cross is the hallmark of that intransigent human rebellion; at the same time, paradoxically, the emblem of the divine love that makes itself vulnerable. That stubborn endurance of irrational hatred is explicable in the assurance that this is God's own world; hence the final victory is his. That is the real meaning of the Christian hope in the final revelation of the Lord Jesus. It is God's creation, disfigured by sin, that will surely be reshaped into a world of his own dimensions.

"Truth Forever on the Scaffold" highlights the problem of personal and corporate evil in the world, a depressing reality, but to be put in the Christian perspective of a final triumph of righteousness, with truth superior to error, love stronger than death.

The Thessalonians had kept their cool in a feverish time. How goes it with us? the preacher may ask. Neither mob riots or lions are real threats to today's Christians. Some of the earlier violence has been exchanged for indifference, society's refusal to take Christianity seriously. Some of it is expressed in ridicule and name calling: ecological freaks; internationalist idiots; social radicals obsessed about hunger, poverty, injustice; enemies of national interests; pious do-gooders. That kind of trouble isn't easy to take either, so many in the churches would rather sing hymns and say their prayers and keep out of sight. The church in Salonika was standing up for Jesus and the gospel in an inhumane society. And

> Still the children wander homeless,
> Still the hungry cry for bread;
> Still the captives long for freedom;
> Still in grief men mourn their dead.

If we, like they, are to show ourselves "worthy of the kingdom of God, for which you are suffering," can the contemporary church ask anything else of the Lord of the church than "Use the love thy spirit kindles, Still to save and make them whole." (See the hymn "Lord, Whose Love Through Humble Service.")

The first reaction to opposition will not be pressing the panic button but strengthened confidence in the rightness of God's cause. "The Cost of Discipleship," "Fools for Christ," "No Easy Way"—suggest sermon titles for this theme. "Becoming Part of the Answer, Not the Problem" is a reminder that though conformity to the world is safer, it only adds to the problem. The Lord doesn't call the church to the principles of "Safety First" but daring investment. A Lenten prayer of confession speaks to us: "Forgive us. Lead us on in life, not into temptation, but transformation, not to safety, but to salvation."

The Final Reckoning (1:7b–10)

In the final reckoning, it is asserted, God's vengeance will fall upon all those who refuse to acknowledge God and upon those who do not obey the gospel. It is worth noting that with all the dramatic fireworks of his description of the divine invasion, Paul pictures the final punishment of the wicked not as annihilation or everlasting torture but as (self-chosen?) exclusion from the presence of Christ (v. 9). The "vengeance" of v. 8 is interpreted as eternal separation from the presence of Christ. The outcome of continued resistance to the purposes of God is the forfeiture of a chance to share in that fellowship with Christ. To be part of that company of Christ is the joy of those who believe the gospel, including these Thessalonian Christians who listened to the first preaching and really heard it (v. 10; see 1 Thess 1:5–8; 2:13).

But does God crush the opposition in the vengeful way Paul imagines (vv. 8–9a)? Is annihilation the only way to deal with the wicked? Paul's anticipation of an eventual subordination, not destruction, of the enemies of God (1 Cor 15:25, 28) and his conviction of a final reconciliation of an alienated creation (Col 1:20) suggest otherwise. In any event the letters surely are devoted far more to the blessed fellowship of God's friends than to the everlasting affliction of his enemies.

Out of his Jewish heritage, interpreted now with reference to Christ, Paul preached an ultimate accountability of every person and people before God. Human history shaped by sin must be appraised by the true Lord of history who is none other than the Creator-Redeemer God. Man is not the measure of all things, as his self-conceit holds, but God and God alone. To Paul the coming of the promised Messiah in Jesus was a sign that the purification of the sin-disfigured world and its reconstitution in the divine design was already under way. The New was now at work in the midst of the Old. In language strongly colored by many apocalyptic symbols from the OT (his Bible), he paints a vivid picture of the Day of Retribution when God's assessment of the man-made world takes place.

In a way without ancient parallel, Israel's thinkers developed an historical consciousness that saw all history as the struggle of humanity with and against God, yet moving ineluctably toward a final God-determined goal. This world of inhumanity and God-defiance must finally be restored to the dominion of God, if God is truly God. For Christians like Paul the church was already the world again become God's domain. Judgment had already begun and was destined to become complete and universal. The "world," this human sphere of conflicting purposes, failures, and disorders, was coming to an end, giving way to a new creation of blessedness and peace in which God's will prevailed. That shattering of human worlds is what happens when God bursts into them.

The themes ringing through this whole discussion of the Last Events are (1) accountability before our Maker, (2) the

victory of righteousness over evil, and (3) punishment as separation from, and its opposite, reward as participation in, that
fellowship. Here are clues to a deeper understanding of a biblical view of judgment that goes beyond the courtroom imagery and torture wracks of traditional Christian preaching. If
the joy of the believer is life with Christ, the penalty of the unbeliever is life without Christ, life which is no-life. Sermon
topics catching up these Pauline themes might include "Vengeance or Reconciliation?"; "Tenants or Landlords?" (emphasizing that as tenants or trustees, we are accountable to
the rightful owner for our lives and for our management of the
earth); "Disadvantaged Lives" (real deprivation is life exclud-
ed from the best of human fellowship and apart from the
Lord).

A Prayer for the Church (1:11–12)

This remarkable praise of the Macedonian Christians who,
despite their uncertainties, are in fact committed to the gospel
(v. 10), finds expression now in a prayer for them all. "May
God count you worthy of his calling, and mightily bring to fulfillment every good purpose and every act inspired by faith, so
that the name of our Lord Jesus may be glorified in you, and
you in him, according to the grace of our God and the Lord
Jesus Christ" (NEB).

The Christian life to which they have been called is always
synergistic, involving human effort and divine assistance. It
called for firm resolves, steady practice, growth in faith and
love on the part of each person. But it was not a solo performance. It was a joint effort. So the completeness of Christian living to which they were called could only be possible by the
power of God at work in them. That's why Paul's exhortation
to moral uprightness invariably climaxes in prayer. Practice
faith and God will make you faithful. Love one another and
God will amplify that love beyond your best efforts. Every
good purpose and every faith-inspired act are brought to completion by his power (v. 11). Thus they will prove worthy of
God's call (v. 11a; see 1 Thess 2:12; 4:7; 5:24). And all to the
end that Christ may be glorified in them and they in him (v.
12). By their perfection of life, made possible by their own resolute commitment and by the empowerment of the Spirit,
they bring honor and glory to Christ. In turn, they are them-

selves honored because of what Christ has done for them.

"To the glory of God and the service of man." A standard formula for dedicating a new sa ctuary or a guest register or a new steam table in the church kitchen. From time beyond recall worshippers have offered votive gifts to their gods as an expression of gratitude or supplication for help. Paul's prayer strikes a deeper note. It is the total person of the worshipper — the noble purposes, the working faith, the inclusive love — by whom the Lord is praised. The preferable interpretation of the difficult Greek phrase in vv. 10 and 12 "to be glorified in his saints" is clarified in the prayer. Because of what these people are, Christ receives glory and praise. And something new is added: this is a mutual affirmation. *They are affirmed because of him, just as he is affirmed because of them.*

That's the wonder of the God of Jesus Christ who not only receives glory but bestows it, who is not only blessed by his worshippers but blesses them. As nobodies we come before his presence to give glory, laud, and honor, and discover ourselves to be somebodies. It is the testimony of experience that in finding God we find ourselves. "In Finding, Found." The passage might be brought into relationship with Gal 4:9: "Now you have come to know God, or rather to be known by God." So you glorify the Lord Jesus and you are glorified.

A Corrective to Instant Victory: Measuring the Opposition (2:1–12)

The Christians in Salonika may have been holding their own against outside opposition, but they were confused and disturbed about the approach of God's Victory Day. Something that Paul wrote, or preached, or declared under the inspiration of the Spirit had been construed by some enthusiasts to mean that the great Day was already dawning (v. 2). Henry Cadbury, brilliant Quaker NT scholar, once described the situation in the Thessalonian church as "over-conversion." The joy and excitement of the new life in Christ may have prompted them to conclude that everything in God's plan was happening at once.

Here, at Corinth, and probably elsewhere, the missionary teacher had to temper the runaway excitement of those who looked for instant victories, instant salvation, immediate triumph over all their troubles. With some sarcasm, Paul described the Corinthian enthusiasts: "Already you have everything you need! Already you are rich! You have become kings, even though we are not! Well, I wish you really were kings, so that we could be kings together with you" (1 Cor 4:8 TEV). Like others since then, they were ready to try on their crowns before they had learned to shoulder the cross.

Not so fast, the apostle counsels. You misunderstand what I told you. You and I are expecting the New Age and we must affirm the reality of that hope, but that doesn't mean that the battle against evil is won before the confrontation happens (v. 3). Entrenched wrong doesn't collapse that easily. You don't understand the dimensions of the problem of a no-God society, nor even the ways of God in righting these wrongs if you think so.

But have we misunderstood the text in v. 2 and hence the underlying situation? The words describing the condition of the community may be translated "easily disturbed" and "in a state of nervous excitement." That may suggest panic rather than Praise-the-Lord enthusiasm. Both emotional responses were probably present. Some were jubilant in their belief that the New Age had begun and the return of the Lord was momentary. Others, confused and alarmed, may have been among those the apostle referred to earlier as the faint-hearted (1 Thess 5:14). For them joy was subdued by the fear that they might not qualify. How can one be sure of the promises of salvation? What if they were denied entrance at the last moment?

If so Paul would have faced the problem of modern preachers. How do we affirm the Christian hope in the face of doomsday prophecies? The first century church was surely not alone in its confusion about how the coming Day of the Lord related to their present condition. This letter gives us guidance. To those with a low self-image and worried about their own future, the apostle urges: Trust that your call is genuine. Believe that God loves you. So the word came to both the cockily confident (enthusiasts) and the nervously depressed (faint-hearted). So the word today must address both the self-assured and the self-depreciative.

What follows in his attempted explanation (vv. 3–12) may have been as mystifying to those Greek friends as it has been for Christians ever since, although he does speak of previous instruction (v. 5) and their knowledge of these things (v. 6a). Augustine's comment in *The City of God* echoes our own feelings.

> Since he said that they knew, he was unwilling to say this openly. And thus we, who do not know what they knew, desire and yet are unable even with effort to get at what the apostle meant, especially as the things which he adds makes his meaning obscure. . . .I frankly confess I do not know what he means (XX, 19).

Of course we recognize the imagery and the basic themes that marked apocalyptic thought of the day, but exactly what Paul had in mind by the Lawless One, Mystery of Lawlessness, the God-imposter, the Restraining (or Controlling) Power, destined to be done away with finally, we can only guess. Would he have been disappointed, I wonder, that these cryptic allusions would become occasions for further fancy and speculation to solve the mystery of God's future and fitting it to human hopes? We can only hope so.

The structure of his teaching is clear. The Day of the Lord will be preceded, he tells them, by the disclosure of a major power of evil (vv. 3– 4, 9– 10a), now temporarily restrained by some supernatural means until the appointed time (vv. 6, 7), which will deceive many people (vv. 3, 10-12). With that terrifying manifestation will come an intensification of evil that is prelude to the day of judgment and the coming of the Lord.

All this however, relates to those who are in the grip of evil and its operation in the world. Condemnation there must be for those who refuse to accept the truth essential for salvation (v. 12), but the faithful must rejoice that they are destined not for condemnation but salvation (vv. 13– 14). That is God's promise.

Perplexed about detail, we can surely track out Paul's directions and pay attention to his convictions, woven into the apocalyptic embroidery. Is he really telling us that the Russians are coming and we'd better be prepared for this "mystery of lawlessness"? That would surprise early Christians who believed that the lawlessness was already at work in the Roman Empire of their own time. Is he urging Praise-the-Lord Christians in the Macedonian capital to face the un-

welcome facts of the power of evil at work in the world, and
yet to reach its apogee? Is he differentiating the cry of God's
people for deliverance, "How long, O Lord, how long?" from
the imperious command, "Hurry up, Lord. Get it done this
very instant!"?

Or is he denouncing the human obstinancy to the gospel,
the stubborn refusal to believe, to love, and to obey its truth,
and the preference to build security and hope upon a delu-
sion? So many exchange the truth for the lie. So many accept
a make-believe reality. Given this state of affairs, we may per-
ceive what Paul means by saying that he has to complete
"what remains of Christ's afflictions" (Col 1:24), instead of
running around shouting "We've won; we've won!" like the
Thessalonian radicals. Paul, too, lives in the joyous expectation of God's New Age. But he believes it doesn't happen magi-
cally; only after major confrontations that involve struggle,
suffering, rebellion, and deception before truth triumphs and
unrighteousness is unmasked.

Meanwhile the Thessalonians and modern Christians must
beware of underestimating the power of evil that frustrates
the full triumph of God. Of becoming so preoccupied with the
hoped-for victory of Christ that they are insensitive to his
presence now. Of objectifying the enemy without—in an immoral society—so that they are oblivious to the enemy within
and hence to the daily need for repentance and forgiveness.
Our Hallelujah-shouts must not conceal our need of penitence, "God have mercy upon us, sinners."

Basic issues of moral man in an immoral society are im-
plicit here. There's a sermon here on "Measuring the Opposition." No one has deeper perception into the diabolical forces
at work in modern society than the Jewish teacher-prophet
Elie Wiesel. He warns us all of the suffering, evil, madness, silence everywhere that threatens to consume our poor world. If
we hear Paul, we cannot understand redemption without participating in that suffering. The story of vast human misery
and suffering must be told, and heard, if redemption can begin to be possible: "Salvation Through Suffering."

Modern rational, technological human beings continue to
be fascinated by secular saviors. Think of the contemporary
vogue of cartoon and TV super-villians and super-heroes.
Compare with those myths the NT hope of Christ's interven-

tion into a satanized world. Does even he picture drawn in 2:1–12 need correction by the teaching of Jesus, as Robert Jewett holds in *Jesus Against The Rapture?* What about a sermon on "Jesus Christ and the Super-Heroes"?

The Confidence of Hope (2:13–15)

After these sharp strictures against those who defy God, the pastor reiterates his thanks and his love for these good friends. "Beloved of God" he called them in the previous letter (1 Thess 1:4); here they are named "Christ-beloved" (v. 13)—a way of referring to the church as the people of God. Reprimand and correction are usually given in the context of appreciative and affirmative love, not, to be sure, for reasons of tact and diplomacy but out of the conviction that they are indeed chosen and called by God despite their foibles. Depending upon the form of the text chosen in v. 13, we may read this as a call "from the beginning of time (*ap'arches*)," that is, the eternal purpose of God's plan of salvation, or as a call to them as "the first converts in the area (*aparchen*)." In either case it is a reminder again of whose they were, a people gathered by God, a people now experiencing and yet to know the full reality of salvation (v. 14).

Once again they are reminded that he is simply clarifying and reinforcing what he had taught them earlier (v. 15). What were these instructions referred to here, in 2:5, again in 3:6 and in the earlier letter (1 Thess 4:1, 2)? Evidently they included an account of the Christian life-style ("how you ought to live" 1 Thess 4:1, see 2 Thess 3:6, 1 Cor 11:2), and expositions on the Christian Hope (2 Thess 2:5), from which we may conclude that both ethical and theological matters were dealt with. And it must be added that these injunctions were not particularly Pauline, but constituted a body of teaching within all the churches of the first century.

Christian education was central and crucial in the early churches. How does that compare with the priorities of twentieth century churches? Not much is said here about prayer meetings and church suppers, or even rummage sales. But there is no mistaking that this is a group of learner-practitioners, called to think through and reorder their human relationships "in the Lord," and to clarify their theological beliefs. And this, not to be better informed, but to let their convictions

shape their conduct. Education, in the end, was not focussed
in a discussion group, but in an apprenticeship. "Continuing
Education in the Church" might point up the literal meaning
of *discipulus* as pupil, learner, apprentice, and emphasize that
Christians ought to be life-long learners. The text in v. 15
"stand firm and hold to" also assumes that education is not
limited to theological reflection but calls also for action training. This is surely "Learning in Living."

A Prayer for the Church (2:16–17)

A fourth little prayer for believers. The NEB translation
captures it beautifully: "May our Lord Jesus Christ himself
and God our Father, who has shown us such love, and in his
grace has given us such unfailing encouragement, and bright
hopes, still encourage and fortify you in every good deed and
word!" God through Christ, the unwearying Giver of wondrous love, unfailing encouragement, and bright hopes. In the
context of this community's problems, Paul bespeaks for them
a confidence that neither persecutions nor death nor confusions about the Final Events, can prevent the true believer
from having part in the future glory. More than that, he prays
that this eternal encouragement will not only give them inner
reassurance of salvation (v. 17a) but empower them to righteous words and actions (v. 17b). Not simply balm to an ach-
ing heart but leverage to performance. Language and
behavior are to be implicated, not only the mind and the
heart.

Love, encouragement, and hope—three great gifts from
God coming to the aid of the weary and the hopeless. They can
become themes for a sermon on "God Our Help and Hope."
The reference in v. 17 to both inward consolation as God's response to prayer and also support for every worthwhile word
we speak and work we do might be developed further in a sermon on "An Alternate Source of Energy: Prayer." It is to be
recognized that true prayer not only brings inner peace and
quiet; it ought also to galvanize us to resolute action for the
Kingdom.

Idling Adventists
(2 Thessalonians 3:1–18)

Words of Encouragement (3:1–5)

This section of the letter (3:1–15) probably is directed especially to the idlers and troublemakers mentioned in the former letter (1 Thess 4:11–12; 5:14). Concluding his encouragement to the fainthearted (1:3–2:17), Paul now prepares to give counsel to the idlers (3:6–15) by first asking for their prayers.

A prayer has been offered for the church in Salonika. Now prayers are requested from the community for the success of the mission in Corinth where the mission team is now working. "Pray for us," Paul asks. He needs their support even as they need his. What does he ask for? Safe passage and personal protection in what continues to be a hazardous environment, for there is strong opposition to his work. There are "wrong-headed and wicked men" (v. 2), perhaps a Jewish reactionary group, that continue to make life difficult for the missioners of the word. But notice that prayers for personal safety don't take first place on Paul's prayer list. First of all he wants them to pray for the speedy and victorious progress of the gospel through the land. "Pray with me that the word gets around" (lit., runs its course; i.e., without being restricted, v. 1). That's the first and foremost concern—not his health and welfare.

Reflect on that familiar phrase Paul uses: "The word of the Lord." Many who read it identify it instantly with the Holy Book. What else is the Word of God? Much else, it may be replied. The apostle is not talking about broadening the circulation of the Scriptures. Here and elsewhere he is not referring to a book at all, which could only have been the Jewish scriptures at this early stage in Christian history. We may recall, at this juncture, that we have already heard Paul speak of the word (1 Thess 1:5, 6); the word of the Lord (1 Thess 1:8, 4:15; 2 Thess 3:1); word of God (1 Thess 2:13); to which we should probably add "the truth" (2 Thess 2:10, 12, 13; see Col 1:5). In all those instances, with the possible exception of 1 Thess 4:15, Paul is speaking of the gospel, the message of salvation in Christ, the content of the preaching in which he and all of them are engaged. The "word of the Lord" in 1 Thess 4:15 is usually taken as a citation or an allusion to a saying of Jesus.

Here are new insights into the nature and the purpose of Christian preaching. There is no demeaning of the task for this man. There is no confusion with the role of the Greek orator of that day. Its real parallel would be the synagogue sermon. Preaching is, quite simply, the spoken word of the gospel, inspired by Christ. It is the whole story of God's seeking and saving the world of humanity, declared by the prophets and realized in Christ, enacted in the preacher. When it is "received" and "believed" it is the deed of human redemption done all over again. That is the word of salvation which is getting around.

Thinking about the story the Acts of the Apostles tells of how the Good News got from Jerusalem to Rome, Professor T. R. Glover once observed that it was gossiped across the Empire. The story was told by full-time missionaries, like Paul, Silas, and Timothy, but also by business people, slaves, travelers, farmers, and housewives, house to house, village to village, city to city, spreading in widening circles. Paul described it in 1 Thessalonians as having "sounded forth" like a trumpet blast (1 Thess 1:8); here he speaks of it as "speeding on" (v. 1) like a runner in a race. The images may inspire sermonic development of the word as the good news of salvation by God's grace, present and powerful in preaching, but active in countless other ways in which the story can be told. It cannot be circumscribed to the pulpit. That word, Paul is fully convinced, will finally triumph. A sermon on "A Multimedia Presentation" might deal with different ways the gospel as power is released into action.

The prayer of dominant desire in this passage centers in the spread and success of the gospel, not personal safety. The Christian taught by the Spirit (Rom 8:26–27) must learn what it means to pray first "thy kingdom come" before he or she asks "deliver us from evil." That might be expressed in a sermon on "First Place on Our Prayer Lists" or "Prayer List Priorities."

Vv. 3–5. Paul moves quickly from concern about himself

and the situation he faces in Corinth to the Thessalonian community. And again it is affirmation and encouragement. Don't worry. God can and will strengthen you against the Evil One, he tells them (v. 3). He is sure (or is he?) they will follow his instructions (v. 4; see 2:15). Earlier (1 Thess 4:2) he had mentioned these Rules for Christian Living which he said he had given them "in the Lord," or "through the Lord," that is to say by the authority of Christ himself. Thus he prepares to make further clarification of what was expected from them (note vv. 6–15). At true followers they were under orders.

Some of them may have complained that too much was asked of them. He seems to anticipate their objection and responds with a brief prayer "May the Lord direct your hearts towards God's love and the steadfastness of Christ!" (v. 5 NEB). Christ will give them the strength they need (v. 3). God's love for them and Christ's endurance can sustain them.

All this may smack of a new legalism to people of today's open and liberated society. "Get off my back; I'll do what I want" is the protest of our permissive society. Even in the church we tend to resist obligations laid upon us. We prefer to make up our own theology rather than learn it from others. Some insist on the right to define "gospel" on their own terms, a personally-acceptable choice among the commandments. "Defining Discipleship"—there's much here to be redone for God's people in a no-God society—and Paul can give us some help.

The Right-And-Responsibility to Work (3:6–13)

Not one to be content with generalized exhortations, Paul proceeds to specify precisely what is involved in obeying orders. Reading the letter as if for the first time and imagining some inspired rules for holy living about to be offered, we might well be shocked by the blunt, mundane precept: "Whoever does not want to work is not allowed to eat" (v. 10). We probably wouldn't include this among any quotations of inspirational sayings by spiritual leaders. Yet there it is, unmistakable and unavoidable, as common and earthy as "Straighten up your room or no supper" or "No more first class flights or gourmet meals at the company's expense."

We remember an earlier allusion to an embarrassing problem in the Salonika community. Some members had claimed a right not-to-work an were not only unproductive (1 Thess

5:14), but had become troublemakers, meddling in other people's affairs (1 Thess 4:11–12) and making general nuisances of themselves. Learn to live quietly, Paul had urged. Keep calm and be self-supportive rather than a burden upon other people. Evidently it didn't do much good for he now addresses himself to the perennial problem of the free-loader with a strong reprimand.

Who were these disorderly misfits in the group? Apocalyptic fanatics? It may be. Extremists who took literally the voluntary poverty Jesus spoke about when he criticized the preoccupation with daily necessities (Matt 6:31)? Possibly. In any event their conduct as well as their convictions had proven more and more disruptive to harmonious life in the community. "We hear that some of your number are idling their time away, minding everybody's business but their own" (v. 11).

What is the basic position? Each one is to work quietly for his own livelihood (v. 12). No ablebodied person has a right to expect others to take responsibility for his support. That, he reminds them, is nothing new. It was one of the rules laid down when the community was first organized (vv. 6b, 10a). But how do you handle the problems created by the persistently non-cooperative? (1) Have nothing to do with them (vv. 6, 14). (2) Follow the example of self-support the mission team set (vv. 7–9). (3) Apply social sanctions in a spirit of fraternal concern for the offender, not out of hostile reprisal (v. 15; see 1 Thess 5:14). Not only the *community*, but also the *miscreants*, must be protected and restored.

We need to handle these texts honestly and accurately. This is *not* a first century criticism of unemployment, workmen's compensation, strikes, and labor unions. It is an impossible exegesis which argues from this primitive social system that *all* poverty is self-willed, a product of a welfare mentality which should be countered not with food stamps but denial of support. The implication in the letters is that these disruptive persons were perfectly capable of supporting themselves but refused to accept that responsibility, busying themselves instead by meddling in other persons' affairs, compounding the problems they were creating. The letters say nothing about others who were incapable of earning their own living.

Community building is a task that must involve the best efforts of each and every member of the group. Vigorous community life requires its members to be producers as well as consumers. And those who persist in doing their own thing rather than participating in the common goals must expect to face disciplinary sanctions imposed by the group. Leadership must model the kind of life-style that makes for community building. So Paul doesn't have to be embarrassed about any personal privileges he ever sought or was granted. He can remind them of how he had waived any apostolic prerogatives, insisting on paying his own way with them. They had set the style. Life together, he will argue elsewhere, is a paradoxical mixture of shouldering the burdens of others (social support) and carrying one's own load (self-support) (Gal 6:2, 5).

It may have been a bit of good old workshop morality Paul utilizes, but the principle of individual contribution to the common good is foundational to any effective group life. It should be noted also that while the loafers are singled out for special reprimand for continuing to disobey his explicit instructions, the discussion is addressed to the whole church (the brethren of v. 6). The responsibility for the peace of the group is laid upon the whole congregation. They cannot avoid the problem, and complaint is not enough. It may be that some of the group had become impatient and harsh in their attitude to these shirkers, ready to give up on them. So we may understand Paul's entreaty, "My friends, don't give them up; don't despair; keep trying to help them," behind the words "Brethren, do not be weary in well-doing" (v. 13).

The passage leads to many possibilities for preaching. It's a long distance between the socioeconomic problems of a tiny first-century group of Greek Christians and those of affluent western nations of the late twentieth century, but it's not unbridgeable. Consumerism, the insatiable appetite for things, is common to both societies. When Pope John Paul II said in New York in 1979, "Christians will want to be in the vanguard of those who wish to cut back on consumerism," he spoke to the Salonika free-loaders and the greedy nations who grow fat and lazy at the expense of others. A sermon might use this Salonika situation to deal with the international problems of gluttonous consumption under the title of "Criteria for Responsible Consumption." In an inequitable world system like ours, Christians ought to be ready to consider a voluntary re-

duction in foods and fuels in the name of Christ and humanity
to make possible a fairer distribution of these basic commodi-
ties among the people of the world. That could be reinforced
with Jesus' words to the rich man, "Sell all that you have, and
give it to the poor" (Mark 10:21). The society that refuses to
imagine this as a duty may finally be disciplined, like the
Salonika insurgents, by a deprivation forced upon it by other
nations in the world community.

We might come at the text from another angle entirely.
Group life always faces the threat of disruption occasioned
by persons who want to play the game by their own set of
rules. They will not accept the objectives and procedures
agreed upon by the others. They claim their rights to alternative ways, yet they want to be part of the group and draw
upon the collective resources. Menonites and Methodists of
the class-meeting era developed covenants governing relationships within their groups which could not be violated
without serious consequences. If those group codes are fault-
ed as overly severe and strict, what is to be said about free-
wheeling societies, including churches, which lack standards and sanctions for the regulation of group life? The
Salonika experience invites careful study to help determine
the meaning of "Responsible Group Participation" for modern church life. We could take another look at Matthew 18 to
discover a very early form of church order that may speak to
contemporary needs.

Managing Conflict in the Church (3:14–15)

What if all these stern reminders and rebukes fall on deaf
ears? What if the troublemakers insist on a confrontation?
How are they to be dealt with? Denounced? Dismissed? Ignored? Tolerated? Reduced rations had been a tactic in the
Dead Sea community of Covenanters to deal with disobedi-
ence. Further discipline called for separation from the Purity
of the Many. It is just this second stage in community sanctions that the apostle now endorses: "Have nothing to do with
that person" (v. 14).

Ostracism from the group is stiff treatment. Later in the
church it would be refined and elaborated into a system of ex-
communication from the sacraments and fellowship. However, the peremptory character of Paul's command is

mitigated by an additional word that provides a vital clue to his understanding of disciplinary measures in the church. "I do not mean treat him as an enemy, but give him friendly advice, as one of the family" (v. 15 NEB). Discipline is not to be punitive, but educative, with rehabilitation as its object.

We're still trying to comprehend that—in society and in the church. Much of our penal code is still fashioned on the medieval notion of societal revenge upon the wrongdoer. Get tough. That's the answer many propose to the mounting problems of crime in our society. Violence can only be met by violence. The church, driven by vague memories of the Inquisition and Puritan witch hunts, on the other hand, has tended to relinquish any form of discipline. At bottom, both church and state often appear to be confused about the nature of community: how to build it, how to set goals, how to manage conflict and threat to community life, how to avoid the extremes of authoritarianism on the one hand and anarchy on the other.

Paul opens up some important insights into any society which intends to take love and justice seriously. Not infallible, to be sure, nonetheless he has keen perception into the new freedom in Christ as living (a) under the guidance of the Spirit and (b) for the community and its life in mutual service. For him the test of every valid ministry, every relationship, every claimed gift of the Spirit is whether or not the community is built up (1 Cor 14:1–19). In a Christian community growing up to the full stature of Christ, one must learn to deal with the weak as well as the strong, the conservative and the radical, the disobedient and the faithful. We're all involved in underdeveloped societies (why do we restrict that to national and economic status?), striving to come to maturity. "In Christ"— never forget it—is essentially a formula for relationships in a community.

If we reflect on these observations, insight and imagination are easily kindled to identify new sermon themes: "Problem Persons and Community Concerns"; "I Don't Want to Play!" (trying to discover the reasons for anti-social conduct before one invokes punishment); "Retaliation or Rehabilitation?" (what difference does it make to regard a wrongdoer as an erring brother or sister rather than an enemy of the people?).

Farewells and a Blessing (3:16–18)

The letter is brought to conclusion with a prayer for peace, an autograph, and a benediction. The expression "God of peace" or "Lord of peace" is used in the letters only in the farewell to the readers (v. 16; see 1 Thess 5:23). Along with other features it suggests a liturgical character to these epistolary greetings and farewells, reminding us of the use of the letters in worship services from the earliest time.

Back of the apparent convention is the wealth of meanings associated with the biblical understanding of peace as *shalom*. For Paul that historic Hebrew concept had been enhanced and given new meaning by all that happened in the event of Christ. *Shalom–eirene* is understood Christologically. So he can now pray for the peace which has its shape and power in Christ the Lord to be bestowed upon this confused and divided little congregation. We must penetrate the words to recognize that something quite specific is prayed for. Peace is seen to be Christ's gift to his people. It is understood to be a protective power, guarding the congregation from inner and outer evils, a source of salvation and blessing which can influence the whole range of inter-human relationships. It is Christ's living presence dwelling with the whole congregation.

Put this passage in relationship with other peace texts in Paul's writings. God *wills shalom*, not disorder in their group life (1 Cor 14:33). Each person is called to live peaceably with others (Rom 12:18). Peace and the building up of the common life are marks of true community (Rom 14:19).

One wonders whether there is a special force to the repeated phrase "with you all" (v. 16b) in the present passage. Paul has been dealing with a dissident minority group of eschatological enthusiasts in terms of relationships with the total community. Now, he seems to say, I cherish Christ's gift of peace for *all* of you, you who are posing problems and you who must take responsibility for the problem makers. His peace is a reconciling, integrative force that mends broken relationships, redefines common goals, and fosters a wholeness of being which is the very nature of salvation (vv. 16, 18).

Then he appends his personal signature to the scribe's work to verify the authenticity of the letter (v. 17, perhaps alluding to the possibility of forged letters which have begun to circulate, as some would have it, see 2:2). He's finished for the time being. This is a certified original; nothing counterfeit, he writes. Here's my hand on it! And the letter is done with the final blessing (v. 18; see 1 Thess 5:28).

A study of Pauline peace texts will yield new sermonic possibilities in the continuing nurture of our congregations. One might develop a message based on these several peace texts under the title "The Peace Which Surpasses Understanding" noting that peace in the NT is (1) God's eschatological peace *given* to humanity, (2) reconciliation, in Pauline usage; something far more comprehensive than the absence of war, or mental tranquillity, (3) a protective power granting harmony and blessing. Another sermon might emerge from the simple but significant realization that the troublemakers, though censured, are still regarded as brothers and sisters who are prayed for: "The Lord be with *you all;* Christ be with *you all.*" It might be titled "Loving Them Through" or "Love Gathers Us In."

PHILIPPIANS

Introduction: Getting Clued In

The Roman military colony of Philippi was another of the Macedonian cities visited by Paul and his mission team on their first travel through the province (Acts 16:20–40). The obscure little village of Krenides, to which Philip of Macedon had given his name when he rebuilt it, was an important administrative center in Roman times. It had been a flourishing gold-mining area in the Hellenistic period and yielded some precious metal under Roman operations. Here in Colonia Julia Augusta Victrix Philippensium was a little Christian group which had been established by the missionaries. Like its neighboring congregation in Salonika, it was struggling to survive against external opposition and internal threats of disunity. That the community had a special place in Paul's affection is evident in this letter as the veteran missionary worker expresses thanks for their generous care and support (Phil 4:14–18; cf. 2 Cor 11:9).

Whether now in Ephesus, as some think, or in Caesarea, as others argue, or in the imperial city of Rome, as most imagine, Paul is no longer a free man but a prisoner of the state, on the eve of a judicial decision which will either acquit him and give him freedom to revisit his friends in the city (1:25, 27; 2:24) or convict him of being an enemy of the state, a crime punishable by death (2:17). In this grave situation he writes a message to be carried by a messenger from the Philippian church, a certain Epaphroditus, who has been delayed by seri-

ous illness but is now recovered and returning to his home
church.

Paul takes advantage of the opportunity to send personal
greetings to dear friends, to give his own account of his situation to supplement the oral report Epaphroditus will certainly make. He tells them that in a strange paradox of
circumstances his own imprisonment is actually resulting in
publicizing the gospel and in winning new interest and enlist-
ment in Christ's cause. Personally he is prepared for a negative verdict by the imperial court and ready for the
opportunity death provides for a reunion with his Lord. Nevertheless he would welcome the chance, if God wills it, to continue the ministry that has been his life work. For some time
he has had no direct contact with the church at Philippi. So it
has been a special joy to receive their deputy, Epaphroditus,
who brought gifts from the congregation, and bolstered his
own weary spirit by the assurance of their love and concern
for his welfare.

The letter must have been penned in the later period of
Paul's career, perhaps between A.D. 58–60 and likely in Rome.
One senses the reflective viewing of a mature career, the reso-
lution to accept in faith the outcome of the present court trial,
the joy of an aging father in his spiritual children, the indomi-
table spirit that refuses to succumb to defeat in prospect of the
final victory. Other letters had likely been exchanged with
this congregation (3:1, 18), as Bishop Polycarp testified in his
own letter written to the same church some 75 years later (see
his letter to the Philippians 3:2; cf. 11:3). It has been proposed
that 2 Thessalonians was in fact a letter sent to the Philippians. More recently it is argued that our letter is composite,
containing fragments of three separate notes. For our purposes, however, we shall regard the letter as a single writing
dispatched by Epaphroditus from Rome to Philippi about the
year A.D. 58.

It would be a misconception to regard the letter as a routine thank you note for some presents received, though that is
the immediate occasion for it. This happy circumstance provides a way to address some larger concerns Paul has in mind
and especially some particular matters related to the church
at Philippi. The repetitious use of "one" and the pleas for con-
cord, following the brief summary of his personal affairs,

point to a problem of division in the community which the apostle identifies with a deplorable individual imperialism (2:2). The corrective to the lordly pride and sense of superiority that was one of the unfortunate reactions to the first flush of conversion is given us, he argues, in the ego-deflating example of the Lord Jesus himself. His sovereignty was not claimed in terms of prestige but in a servant relationship to others. He was truly "the man for others" in the simple but compelling Bonhoeffer word. Not averse to specifics, Paul cites two Macedonian women workers in the congregation who have had a falling-out and he appeals to the leader of the group to bring them together (4:2–3).

Division and strife all too often accompany the ambitious teachers who twist the true and only gospel to their own ends, the apostle contends. Several leadership types are referred to without specific identification. Some are accused of preaching Christ "out of partisanship," personally spiteful to the jailed leader (1:14–15). They may be Jewish-Christians of a conservative stripe often encountered in the Pauline churches, or simply fellow-missionaries, Jew or Gentile, who were jealous of the apostle and critical of him. The latter seem to answer to the charges of Paul in 2:21. But it is clear that in 3:1 his attention is directed to conservative Jewish-Christian missionaries who had regularly followed up Paul's work, trying to convince the Gentile converts that circumcision and Torah obedience were enjoined upon all believers in Jesus the Messiah. Their pride in being in the authentic bloodline constituting the people of God finds no support from this Jewish convert to Christ who believes his new existence is made possible unconditionally by what God has done for him in Jesus Christ. And that must be true for everyone.

Other problem persons may be identified in Paul's critical comments about a degenerate secularism that despite their pretensions makes them actually "enemies of the cross of Christ" (3:17–19).

A lifetime of intensive labor rewarded by blessings and blows has taught him how to cope with contradictory experiences. This secret he shares with his friends (4:8–13). Here are some rich reflections of a senior citizen on a life's journey nearing its end that can speak with power and blessing to all of us.

Personal letters have a way of exposing the human heart beyond most other forms of self-expression. As I write, literary reviews are appearing on the monumental Harvard edition of Lord Byron's collected letters nearing completion in a projected twelve volume set. The first volume of a seven volume edition of D. H. Lawrence's letters has just appeared. Here were two giants in letter writing in English. Journals and diaries are also confessional and intimate, perhaps less revealing because of their private intention. But correspondence is an interpersonal act and reveals more of oneself than the writer intends. Do we show ourselves more directly and honestly as we relate ourselves to other persons than we do in the privacy of introspection? It may be. Our letters and our check books (see 2 Cor 9:13, 14) may tell more about us than we are ready to admit. And if one is in the grip of adverse experiences, letters to others may disclose the ranges of personality in a fascinating way.

How do we explain ourselves to others? "Who Do We Think We Are?" Based on Paul's prison letters and his admonition to generosity in giving (the check book), a sermon could be developed on how we explain ourselves to others, deliberately and unconsciously. What kind of messages do we convey? We tell our own story in several ways as we make ourselves known to others and they, in their way, are made known to us.

We are about to explore one of several letters written by Paul from prison to beloved friends. How does a veteran of ministry deal with this unwelcome situation? What is happening to his faith? How does he view his future? What does he have to say to friends who have leaned heavily upon his counsel in the past? Is he remorseful? Vindictive? Despairing? Optimistic?

Other Christians have also had to face such an ordeal. As we listen to the first century missionary, try reading along with it in Dietrich Bonhoeffer's *Letters and Papers From Prison* (1953). Ponder Martin Luther King's "Letter From Birmingham City Jail" (see J. M. Gustafson and J. M. Laney, *On Being Responsible*, 1964, pp. 256–74). What do each of these responses say to us about Christian witness in a secularized social order?

To the Roman Colony of Philippi: From the Blues to a Hallelujah!
(Philippians 1:1–26)

Warm Greetings and a Prayer for the Church
(1:1–11)

Some 9½ miles from the seaport of Kavalla (NT Neapolis) in northern Greece, the modern tourist enroute to Salonika comes upon the ruins of the once grand Roman colony of Philippi, a leading city in the first century district (Acts 16:12). One travels over, and again alongside, the same military road (Via Egnatia) on which Paul, Silas, and Timothy walked on their first visit. Still visible are portions of the old Roman highway that forged a direct link between Rome and the east, eventually as far as Byzantium (Istanbul). With vivid memories of several visits there, Paul and Timothy write to old friends to report on Paul's personal situation and to offer some pastoral guidance on church problems.

This is the only salutation in the extant letters of Paul in which he singles out the church leadership for special mention by title. Interestingly enough, he does not use the common term "elder," but refers instead to the bishops (overseers; note the plural; no monarchical bishop yet!) and the deacons (1:1). Why, we cannot tell. But it is worth noting toward any definition of clergypersons in the NT that these leaders, whatever their roles, are a functional part of the whole church. The individual Christians at Philippi he names as the "separated ones," i.e. "the saints," "a holy people," probably with the language of Exod 19:6 and Deut 7:6 in his ears. It is to them, the total congregation of God's people, that the letter is addressed, with the special officers mentioned secondarily. It is the whole church, not simply the clergy, which is designated as set apart, sanctified, called to share the holiness of God.

In a day when the term Christian is often made synony-
mous with citizen, or non-Jew, it should give us pause and reproach to see how acutely self-conscious the early church was
about its identity. They saw themselves as a minority group,
highly visible to themselves and their neighbors, in a tension
relationship with the larger society of which they were a part.
How can the church in any day fulfil its intended mission in
the world unless it has a clear understanding of itself? What
does it mean to be the church of Christ in the world? The answer to that question will not be found by consulting legal papers, taking a community poll, or examining social statistics.
We must search our own consciences and the scriptures for
that. Here the pulpit has a special responsibility in confronting the congregation steadily with the biblical understanding of the church.

Is it simply a literary convention that leads Paul to address
"all the people of Christ Jesus who are at Philippi" rather than
simply saying "the First Philippian Church"? I think not. He
conceives the church as a totality, one body in Christ, scat-
tered but indivisible. It is as though he writes, "To the one
Church of Jesus Christ as it is localized in Philippi, or in Salonika, or in Corinth." The geography is secondary to and ex-
planatory of the primary Christological reality. One church,
one body, one people. His thought moves from the whole to
the part; ours more often from the part to the whole. The diffi-
culty with the latter, in the history of the church, is that the
part is too easily mistaken for the whole.

Something stupendous might begin to happen to us today
if an international cross-cultural, inclusivist understanding of
church were to be our pre-thought rather than an after-
thought in our planning and practice as Christians. This text
can lead us to search out other clues in Paul's letters about the
real nature and function of the church. Some conclusions for a
series of sermons could be: (1) The church as God's *gathering*
in Christ (a convocation, called into being, divinely initiated
not self-chosen). (2) The wholeness of the church in each of its
parts (one body in Christ, 1 Cor 12:12–27). (3) The church as
an open, inclusivist society (Gal 3:28). (4) The church as God's
delegation in Christ (a witnessing community). (5) The church
as the *avant garde* of the Kingdom (the model in time and
space of true society). (6) The whole church as ministerial (1

Cor 12:4–7). Management and sociological terminologies in vogue today may provide some helpful clues, but they cannot penetrate to the center of the church's reality.

"Thankful for your partnership in the gospel" (vv. 5, 7; see 4:3), your *koinonia*, your sharing with me in the work of the gospel from the very outset of our relationship. Silas, Timothy and many others had served in the traveling mission team with the apostle, but in a basic sense these Philippian Christians had been co-workers with him from the first. It's poor leadership, though widely practiced, that regards the group as spectators. Dynamic leadership recognizes other members as partners in the process, and that not at some suitable stage in their development but alive and at work from the outset.

"What have you been doing?" is the question that is properly put to each of us. And the response, "Well, to tell the truth, we've mainly been watching" is too often the case. The Christian community, alive and well, will make place for very few official observers but succeed in enlisting everyone in outworking rather than on-looking. Attitude inventories are of less worth than performance tests. These friends at Philippi are praised as partners with him in God's wondrous favor— both while he freely defended and demonstrated the gospel, and even now while he languishes in custody (v. 7). Put that together with the identification of Timothy as God's co-worker in 1 Thess 3:2 and you have a good view of church members in partnership in the gospel.

Church membership for Paul was no simple "signing up" but accepting partnership in a staggering task to make the gospel known to all people. "From Spectators to Participants" suggests itself as a sermon theme in which the meaning of membership in the church is explored. Indeed, one wonders if the very phrase "in the church" is non-Pauline. I think he would not speak of being *in* the church but rather *being* the church.

Paul is moved to prayer (vv. 9–11). With pastoral concern, Paul prays that these friends at Philippi will continue in their Christian growth, learning how to love, becoming more knowledgeable and spiritually perceptive (v. 9). He wants them to become more discriminating in determining what is right and good (v. 10). One is struck by the emphasis here upon the nature of love as rational and discriminating in moral choices. This is no namby-pamby lovableness. Professor Marvin Vincent summarizes the passage in a formal way, "May your love increase and abound in ripe knowledge and perceptive power, that you may apply the right tests and reach the right decisions on things which present moral differences" (International Critical Commentary, p. 13). To which I would add, "And thus become fully mature in Christ" (vv. 10b, 11).

Growing up in love has unexpected features, according to Paul. Knowledge and insight alone are not sufficient as guides to decisions, but a knowledge and insight *in the control of love,* the kind of love exhibited in God's act for us all in Christ. The key to it all is that divine love (*agape*) which must "abound more and more." Knowledge, perception, spiritual gifts of every sort (1 Cor 12–14)—all have value as they are exercised *in love,* which is to say, the beneficient effect they have on another's need.

That's an interesting correlation of terms: love, knowledge, perception, prove in practice (RSV prefers the alternative translation, "approve," but the verb carries the sense of actively testing; see Rom 12:2). And all of them are interpretative of what mature love and the Christian life are all about. Clearly love is much more than an emotional thrill. With this passage on the relationship of love, understanding, and discrimination, we might profitably compare the discussion of faith and understanding in 1 Cor 14. They suggest rich possibilities for sermon themes on "Learning How to Love," "Making Right Choices," "Knowledge Isn't Enough!" How strange that many atomic scientists are more urgently trying to say all this than the church appears to be!

His hope for them is that they shall yet become flawless, sure-footed (that is, not stumbling themselves or causing others to trip up; morally upright). This is Christian character as it is possible through Christ (vv. 10b–11). It is life lived "to the glory and praise of God." The new life is not suddenly and completely realized. Instead, he argues continually, it's a process of development including failure and success, moving from infancy ("babes in Christ") to adulthood ("spiritual persons," 1 Cor 3:1). The command to the disciple is never "Rest and relax!" but "Keep moving!" (see 3:12).

An Unexpected Benefit in Personal Suffering (1:12–14)

A moment ago, v. 7, Paul had referred to his personal situation as a man in the custody of the state, a fact already known to his first readers (but a surprise to us). Now he makes reference to the praetorium (v. 13), the special hand-picked troops of the emperor under his direct command. Probably Paul is under house arrest, permitted private lodging under the guard of a praetorian soldier. Here he had been visited by the delegate from the Philippian congregation, Epaphroditus, who is about to leave for home carrying this letter to the church with him. It is not a new situation for the apostle. In an earlier letter to the group in Corinth he had spoken of some of his ordeals, among them "many imprisonments" (2 Cor 11:23) as well as countless beatings which had brought him more than once o death's door, a claim scarcely imaginary since it was verifiable.

But what had been an effort to silence him had boomeranged into a new publicity for the gospel. It wasn't long before others at military headquarters knew that a Jewish prisoner was charged with treason, advertising a new king to be recognized. Indeed the word had spread among the public at large in the city, and emboldened Christian friends were talking freely about their faith in Messiah Jesus to any who would give them a hearing. So Bonhoeffer in Tegel Prison, Buchenwald, Schönberg, and finally Flossenburg; Martin Luther King in Birmingham jail—both men became focal centers of widening notoriety and influence. Persecution for the sake of loyalty to God's kingdom becomes a source of blessing, encouragement, and liberation to others, as the Lord had promised his harrassed followers (Matt 5:10, 11).

When someone backs up his word with his life, people do stop, look, and listen. They don't all become believers, of course. Some taunt; some ridicule; some are perplexed; some pray. The twentieth century Holocaust confronts us all with the reality of Judaism in a new way and the eternal mystery that in death new life is given. Judaism destroyed becomes Judaism re-born, to the fury of its murderers. The vitality of beleagued Christian churches in eastern Europe and the Far East brings under judgment the listlessness of western churches at ease in Zion.

There are other forms of persecution than violence. Movements are not stopped by assault so much as by neglect. Condescending tolerance by society may prove to be more destructive to vigorous church life than drastic action taken against it. That's a hard lesson the church has had to learn through history. But Christian obedience has to be prepared for opposition whether by hostile actions or by indifference. Bonhoeffer wrote, "When Christ calls a man, he bids him come and die." Where Christians have been prepared to be personally expendable for the sake of the gospel, there the church has never died but come to life, and God's truth has gone marching on. "Truth Will Out" suggests itself for sermonic development with special emphasis on how endurance through hardship can become an eloquent witness of faith. Research would be needed, but a sermon on "Martyr Churches of Our Time' could give our congregations a new sense of oneness with oppressed Christians elsewhere.

Every pastor knows at first hand the depth of the the problem of suffering in human experience. He or she must help people deal with it in the thousand ways it invades their lives and threatens to destroy them. The mystery of it remains beyond all our reckoning with it. But the greater meaning is that it is possible for new life to come through suffering. The word of the cross is that even death cannot defeat life. That's what can be heard in v. 12: a man's adversity becomes God's opportunity! Even personal reverses can be used to make advances. Paul's experience here, verified by many a saint of God, is evidence that God can make all things, including misfortune and defeat, to work together to a larger good for those who love and trust him. These perceptions might be gathered together around a sermonic theme such as "Overcoming Defeat" or "Making the Best of the Worst."

Preachers Come in Several Shapes and Sizes (1:15–17)

The restrictions of house arrest must have given the old man plenty of time to reflect on his work to date, the problems that continued to dog his way, the prospects that lay before him. He had known joy in the service of Christ. And he had also experienced frustrations because of fellow missionaries

who differed with his understanding of the gospel and resent-
ed strongly the authoritative leadership that was his style.
Even though the witness of many of the local Christians
continued to be strong and confident (v. 14), Paul had to face
the fact that some of them were resentful of his leadership and
took advantage of his arrest to assert their own authority for
preaching the gospel. Probably these persons are not to be
identified with other opponents who openly denounced Paul
and claimed that his was a perversion of the true gospel by refusing to recognize the centrality of the Mosaic law as well as
Christ in salvation. At any rate the preachers referred to at
this point (vv. 15–17), while criticized for their quarrelsome
and competitive spirit, are still acknowledged as preachers of
Christ. Though he disagrees with their motives he can still be
happy that in some way Christ is still proclaimed through
them. He does not quarrel with the content of their message
but with their attitude and spirit, and the divisive effect it has
on the community. Apparently Paul himself, ever the controversial figure, is the provocation of this partisanship among
the leaders and the people. His reading of the situation is that
they hold a personal animosity against him out of envy of his
leadership and influence. And now that he is less able to defend himself they are creating fresh trouble for him and dissension in the community.

Preachers come in many shapes and sizes. We are not
struck from a single mold. Our backgrounds, training, outlook, aptitudes are different. Our pastoral and preaching
skills vary. Some are specialists in organizational tasks;
others fight losing battles with schedule and program demands. Like other members of our congregations, each of us
has special insights into what the sovereignty of Christ means
for us as persons and as a society. So our emphases vary in the
interpretation of the faith as well as in our leadership styles.

But how do we respond to those who make a practice of ad-
vancing their own cause by demeaning the work of others?
That carping spirit finds expression in inter-denominational
competitiveness; "Christian" forms of anti-Semitism; scram-
bles for leadership posts; feuding congregations; the Electric
Church's vendettas against traditional forms of the church;
and many other ways. Life within the household of faith must
strike many an outsider to be not so much an ordered society

as a civil war. It is a blameworthy fact that we often defend our faith by derogating the faith of others.

Now the passage before us offers us insight into a constructive response to unjust criticism. Paul, as human as the rest of us, often flares up in self-defense against unjustified verbal abuse. In this section, however, we hear none of that defensiveness; only the half-amused comment that "whether in pretense or in truth" Christ is in fact being proclaimed, and, what really matters, the gospel is actually advanced! He has come to an appreciation of those who disparage him! So, he might have added, God neutralizes opposition and makes my personal detractors to praise his name! Now that's a different way of taking criticism!

We might ponder this as we confront tensions in church staff relationships, conflicts in team ministries, committee squabbles, denominational rivalries. Christ may still be proclaimed, though not always in our own style. It is possible, at least, that some of our discussion is not really over the basic matters of the gospel, as we like to think, as it is a personal contest of jarring wills and ambitions. The primary questions to be raised about all our ministries, lay and ordained, are Paul's: Is Jesus Christ proclaimed as Lord of all? Is the congregation built up? Am I prospering? seems to be overlooked in the NT tests of ministry.

A sermon might be developed on "Disarming The Opposition" in which one could contrast the instinctive response of self-defense to criticism to the cheek-turning appreciation of the contribution others are making. Relate Paul's generous affirmation of some of these difficult associates to Jesus' plea for loving enemies and repaying the curse with a blessing (Luke 6:27, 28). Ultimately, for Jesus and for Paul, the source of such extraordinary behavior to which we are enjoined is the Merciful One who is kind to the ungrateful and the selfish. The cross is the sign and seal of that.

Or come at it another way by emphasizing the central significance of the issue at stake (the gospel) rather than personal feelings. Conflict management must be able to disentangle the basic positions from the name-calling, the angry rejections, and bruised feelings if negotiation of differences is to be achieved. Truth may be served in different ways. Some of these elements of problem situations can find embodiment in a single sermon or a series on "Dealing With Controversy."

Prison Blues and New Hope (1:18–26)

Still, personal feelings and personal needs cannot be ignored. In what follows, Paul confesses some prison blues which have plagued him. He permits us a moment's intimate glance into his own heartache and the fresh hope that healed it. At least that is how it may be read. Afflictions there are aplenty. The possibility of personal disgrace and failure has to be allowed. Death in many ways would be a welcome release from all these troubles (v. 23). But that is a selfish wish. Whatever his personal fortunes, whether he lives or dies, he is determined to devote himself completely to preach and be expendable for Christ's sake (v. 20). He had once reminded the Thessalonians, as he now tells the Philippians, that these tough times are evidence of God's righteousness, and of his pledge that we are chosen to live with him. Not to be condemned in judgment but to be accepted. Chosen for salvation not destruction (v. 19; contra RSV, NEB, TEV etc., which understand "salvation" as Paul's release from his present arrest). Whether he lives or dies, that's the way it will turn out; of that he is fully persuaded. We recall his words "that you may be made worthy of the kingdom of God, for which you are suffering" (2 Thess 1:5). What is said to his friends, he must say to himself.

The Jerusalem Bible turns Paul's Greek into English this way: "My one hope and trust is that I shall never have to admit defeat (i.e., be put to shame), but that now as always I shall have the courage for Christ to be glorified in my body, whether by my life or by my death" (v. 20). That's what it means to be worthy of the Kingdom. Never to retract what he has said; never to admit that he was a deluded enthusiast for a fraudulant Messiah. More than ever bold in speech and belief that Christ is the only Messiah and Lord. That is his passionate hope. So it is with the people of God. The more the world tells them to shut up, the louder becomes their shout. We may well ask if the church in our time, faced with all the hostilities of a God-denying society, hasn't developed laryngitis, just when full voice is needed desperately. "Letting Our Voice Be Heard" could be a call to action for the church in a crisis-oriented society.

Looking at the passage again, one is struck by the way in which the personal concerns are subordinated to the needs of

others. Both human weakness and superhuman hope find expression in Paul's plaintive admission, "I want to die and to
be forever with Christ" (v. 23). That would really be "goin'
home." Life has seldom smiled sweetly on this man. It's been
push and shove, struggle and conflict, rebuff and humiliation
all along the way. What a relief it would be to have it all over.
Yet if it should be to the interest of people like these friends at
Philippi that he continue to live and be permitted to carry on
his work, then his personal preferences have no place. Convinced of this, he expects that the way will be found for him to
be freed and to continue his work (vv. 24–26).

Death will not be forced upon this man; he can choose it,
welcome it, anticipate it, not dread it. But even though it is *his*
death, others have a claim upon his life. Paul refuses to succumb to the blues about his personal situation because he has
such a strong sense of responsibility to others. There were
loved ones to be considered; people who needed his ministry.
They couldn't be crowded out while he basked in self-pity or
fantasized his personal future (Oh, that will be glory for me!).
We are talking here about the social effects of personal suffering, a dimension well known to the medical social worker.
"The Greening of the Blues" is a colorful (!) way of discovering
how to break through the Me-centered nature of enveloping
depression by reaching out to the other persons we need and
who need us. Or think of it as "Jail Break."

Much is involved here: gratitude for the prayerful support
of a prisoner by good friends; the determination to be a faithful witness, come what may; death as a doorway to larger life;
the priority of the needs of others over personal advantage—
all become reality in the actual situation of a man fighting for
his life. Each of us must face his own death. Learning how to
live must involve learning how to die. Paul, Bonhoeffer, King
teach us much of both. And each points to the Christ who for
us all is Lord of life and death.

Preparation for death and dying is widely discussed today
in a society that previously has shunned the topic. Seminars
and group discussions are held not o ly in the church but in
schools and community programs with doctors, social workers, lawyers, psychologists and psychotherapists providing
much needed and helpful assistance. Is it possible that the
Christian witness can be crowded out? Does the pastor whose

contribution is solely an examination of rituals involved in the grieving process fulfill his distinctive ministry? The pulpit can become a unique place to declare the theological issues of death and dying and to address them from the standpoint of Christian faith. Can we hear that in these prison reflections of this prisoner?

Afterthought: A sermon on intercessory prayer? It is structured in v. 19: the church praying for the prisoner; the power of the Spirit of Christ; salvation assured. Rejoice!

From Individualism to Interactive Community
(Philippians 1:27–2:30)

Firm in the Faith (1:27–30)

Paul turns from his own situation at this point to consider that of his friends who have troubles of their own. The opposition (v. 28) is unspecified but known well enough to the readers so that Paul fears they may become disheartened and give up. He wants them to stand firm in obedience to all that their new life requires of them. Notice how the term "gospel of Christ" (v. 27) and the unusual phrase "the faith of the gospel" (v. 27) are employed with reference not to a set of doctrines but to their whole way of life. The gospel for Paul was not a creed, or a set of propositions, but a total life-style. Indeed in the passage he uses a striking expression, found nowhere else in his letters. It is translated "manner of life" in most versions but its literal meaning is "exercise your citizenship." It reminds us of the cognate term in 3:20 which speaks of a Christian commonwealth. It was natural enough for Paul, like the Stoics, to use Roman imperial imagery to define the role of the believer as a citizen in the new commonwealth of Christ the King. They are to be good citizens in every sense.

They are called to united action as a single person in mind and spirit against the opposition. There is a hint already of some disarray in the Philippian ranks in the way that oneness is emphasized. We shall hear more about this. The Thessalonians had been told that their struggles for survival in a hostile environment were evidence that they were being tested and fitted for God's kingdom (2 Thess 1:5). So now the Philippians are reminded that a Christian front in undivided loyalty to Christ and in obedience to the demands of their new citizenship is evidence that they are destined for salvation while the opposition is headed for ruin (v. 28). The pledge of salvation is evident in the privilege conferred upon them of suffering for his sake (v. 29). They are partners with Paul in the same struggle he faced with them in Philippi and which he now faces in Rome (v. 30).

We still continue to reduce the gospel to a set of theological statements in the face of the repeated insistence of the NT that the response to God's act on our behalf is a new kind of being and doing—not just thinking. We are called into a new life-world that requires human transformation, not a rearranged belief system. That is what we are hearing from Paul in this account of the gospel as a "manner of life" or a "citizenship to be exercised." Salvation is not simply a gift handed to us; it is something to "work out . . . with fear and trembling" (2:12). Homiletically that might be developed on the theme of "Achieving Salvation" as a corollary to another sermon on "Accepting Salvation." In the "something for nothing" disposition of our contemporary society, it is a necessary if uncomfortable word the preacher must speak along with the apostle, "Avoid anything in your everyday lives that would be unworthy of the gospel of Christ" (1:27 JB).

That kind of discipleship may very well put us at cross purposes with the society we live in, as it did the Philippians and their friend Paul. Conflict and struggle is the very nature of the attempt to live a godly life in a no-God world. All Paul can offer is an invitation, Don't stand to the side and watch. Get into the fight! (1:30). "Who is on the Lord's Side?" could raise the issue of the tension between the church and the world with the development of the theme along three lines: (1) The variance of Christ's way with society's way; (2) Reconciling love rather than violence as the Christian arsenal; and (3) The privilege of sharing with Christ in his suffering for the world.

Some "I" Problems (2:1–4)

Now the problems of partisanship (1:17) and dissension in the Philippian church begin to be more apparent as the apostle commences an intense appeal for a peaceful and unified community. We hear of rivalry, conceit, superiority feeling as threats to the community (v. 3). It was a common problem in these younger churches, as Paul's letters testify. Perhaps one of the first reactions to the experience of liberation among converts was a new sense of self-worth and pride denied them by birth and upbringing in their Roman society. This may have led to pretensions to elevated status and special knowledge, as in Corinth (1 Cor 1–4) that encouraged an ego strength detrimental to community life. At any rate the apostle is much concerned about the matter and speaks at some length about it.

If your new life in Christ has given you any encouragement for life together—if there is any persuasive power in love—if you have experienced any real *koinonia* or participation in the Spirit—if you have discovered what tenderness and compassion for one another mean—then, make me really happy by being united in mind and agreeing in love, shunning divisive ambitions and petty contentions. That appeal for unanimity of mind (2:5) employs the same word, "be minded," as we find repeatedly in 1:7; 3:15, 19 and 4:2. Obviously he holds this kind of loving agreement essential to true community whereas self-seeking and rivalry are destructive.

Paul is not one to be content with generalities. To have a disposition oriented toward others rather than self is laudable enough, but it's like approving reverence or altruism. What specifically does it mean? What does it look like in practice? He is ready for our questions and begins an explanation that will be developed over the next sections. "You should humbly reckon others better than yourselves. You must look to each other's interest and not merely to your own" (vv. 3–4 NEB). Taken by itself the first might be understood as an endorsement for an inferiority complex, a low self-esteem that is inimical to personal growth. It becomes clear in context that Paul is not talking about unhealthy self-derogation, but of a meekness and modesty that are expressed in primary concern for the welfare of others. It is the very opposite of arrogance and self-righteousness. It has nothing in common with an over-anxious attitude of "How am I doing?" or personal pulse-taking. He would find the militant ego theories of a Nietzsche or Ayn Rand alien to the gospel.

For this advocate of Christian community vs. pious individualism, sin is essentially the violation of a brother or sister's need. His is first and last a social view of the human person. It is, I think, a mark of the culture-conditioning of a Me-first society that leads us to misread Paul as an individualist talking of personal salvation, when, for him, to be "in Christ" is shorthand for being "in the body of Christ," i.e., being-in-relation-to-others, centered-in-Christ.

"Taking a New Look at Yourself" might be the subject of a

sermon moving out of this text which probes the difference between valuing everything in terms of self-interests and valuing others and their concerns above our own. "The Gospel and
the Me-Generation" would be an alternate subject. But we
must listen further to Paul's analysis of the new disposition or
mind-set before we are prepared to deal adequately with this
basic Christian life orientation.

An Ancient Hymn to Christ: The Model of Humble Obedience (2:5–11)

Paul really invents the Christian meaning of the secular
Greek work *tapeinophrosyne*, commonly translated "humility." The dictionary meaning is meanness of spirit or lowness
of rank. In Christian use, however, it characteristically referred to self-effacement, the "littleness" of the child, in a favorite image of Jesus. For Paul it is a demeanor that finds its
finest expression in the total reality of the Christ event. If one
asks for a definition, he points not to a lexicon but to a person.
It is probable that the present passage is excerpted from an
early Christian hymn, but, if so, the thought is in accord with
Paul's own view of Christ. It may be divided into three stan-
zas, as J. Jeremias proposes:

I
(Christ), though in the form of God,
Did not count equality with God something to be
grasped,
But emptied himself, taking the form of a slave,
Being born in the likeness of men.

II
And being found in human form,
He humbled himself and became obedient unto death,
even death on a cross.

III
Therefore God has highly exalted him
And bestowed on him the Name which is above every
name,
That in the name of Jesus every knee should bow, in
heaven and on earth and under the earth,
And every tongue confess that Jesus Christ is Lord,
To the glory of God the Father.

(2:6–11; see also 1 Cor 15:47; 2 Cor 8:9)

This beautiful and deeply moving Christ hymn, one of several in the NT, has inspired poets, hymn writers, liturgists, and theologians through the ages. But it is not always understood in the sense of Paul's use of it here. In itself a liturgical expression of the mystery of the incarnation and salvation, it must be noted that it is not intended as a statement of the preincarnate and incarnate modes of Christ's existence, but as the supreme example of self-renunciation and obedience. The whole event of Christ in his coming, in his living and dying, in his triumph, is offered as the model for the true humility which should distinguish human relationships in the church. Rather than seizing hold on that divine status (the form of God, v. 6) he beggared himself by accepting the position of a slave (v. 7), submitting himself finally to a criminal's death (v. 8). But the outcome is the exaltation of Christ, a new role of sovereign leadership, destined to be universally recognized (vv. 10, 11; see Is 45:23).

In the servant life and death of Jesus of Nazareth, faith discovers that it is none other than God himself who is present. God declares himself not in stupendous power nor celestial majesty, but in an insignificant poor man who gives up everything including his life for the sake of others. That is the scandal of the gospel. That is the model of exemplary behavior. That is what it means not to be preoccupied with oneself but to enter lovingly into the lives of others (v. 4).

It is the recurrent theme of Jesus' teaching, of course: the least is the greatest, the humble one the exalted, the last are really the first, the poor are the rich, the meek are the masters, the life-loser is the life-finder, the servant is the leader. But how are we to make it real for our world where self-sufficiency and success are the most prized goals? People like Mother Teresa of Calcutta or Martin Luther King Jr. may evoke admiration from us, but less likely emulation. They seem to be strangers to our culture, visitors from another planet, intruders into the space which is home to us but foreign territory to them. Can we help our folks and ourselves to see that this is only a self-defense, a way of escaping from the call to let our own lives be changed?

The appeal-demand of Paul, after all, is addressed to real persons in a real city, no better and no worse than any one of us. They were: (a) converts whose conversion was only begun;

(b) hostages to a society which honored different values and life-styles than the gospel sets out; (c) eager to praise the Lord without necessarily attempting life-adjustments; (d) grateful for the support of their community as long as it didn't conflict with personal prerogatives. That profile describes contemporary congregations as accurately as it does ancient ones. So it is *we ourselves* who are being addressed, reminded of the pattern of Christ, and informed that our way can only be his way. If he is the "man for others," then we falsify our allegiance if we are not.

The Christ hymn as Paul employs it opens up a number of possibilities of interpreting its basic meanings in preaching. "Demonstrating Discipleship" might reaffirm that true following is not merely affirming but actually doing the will of God. The servant life of Christ is God's *own* act of judgment and love for an alienated world. That might become the theme for a sermon on "The Servant God," a shocking way of conceiving ultimate being. The hymn writer has understood that deep truth:

> Amazing mystery of love!
> While posting to eternal pain,
> God saw His rebels from above
> And stoop'd into a mortal man.
>
> His mercy cast a pitying look,
> By love unbounded, love inclined,
> Our guilt and punishment He took
> And died a victim for mankind.

It is the Everlasting God who enthrones Christ. It is to his glory that the Lordship of Christ is acclaimed. It is God at last who will be "everything to everyone" (1 Cor 15:28). The faith of the earliest Christian communities and the faith of Paul affirm the priority and preeminence of the Father God.

Recognizing the church as a proper experimental center for testing out new kinds of human relationships where "I" is transfigured into "We" might be signaled by the title "The Church as a Counterculture." There are signs all about of a mounting dissatisfaction with our acquisitive consumer society: college students in rebellion creating bizarre counter cultures; business and professional people abandoning lucrative urban posts for less comfortable service-directed vocations, retired persons discovering more meaningful life in non-profit work for the needy. Must we not take more seriously our group life in Christ as a viable alternative to a society which measures its worth by the GNP?

Look again at that extraordinary act of self-renunciation (v. 7). "He beggared himself" (F. W. Beare). He made himself of no account, worthless, insignificant, in terms of what the world holds to be of account, worthy, significant. A Somebody who was willing to become a Nobody. That's the paradox of Jesus. Only a few have been able to take him seriously, let alone literally—an Italian Francis or a Russian Theodosius. We can deal with majesty; but we are nonplussed by humility. We understand pomp and circumstance; we are puzzled by voluntary poverty. Power we can comprehend; love is mystery. Yet it is that strange kind of world over which God is truly king, modeled before our very eyes in the person of Jesus of Nazareth. Our sermon skills will be tried, and we ourselves put to the test, to make that kind of abasement comprehensible and attractive. But the gospel imagery is close at hand: the proudly self-righteous holy man side by side with the sinful publican; the kinds of the world vis-a-vis the little child. How do the stiff-legged learn how to kneel? How does the manipulator learn how to cooperate? How do the great become little? That is the mystery of conversion. "Bigger Is Better—Or Is It?"

Salvation Is a Gift and a Task (2:12– 13)

The appeal has been that the Philippians be in full accord and of a common mind (2:1– 4). The ground of that appeal has been established in the whole reality of Christ's saving work, the humiliated servant who has been enthroned by God as king (2:6– 11). Now, Paul urges, you are to be so minded (v. 5). In sum, you are to accomplish your salvation, knowing that it is God who wills and works through you to that end.

If salvation is at the very center of the Christian good news, then this must be a passage of primary importance to each of us who tries to make real the Christian experience of salvation. Jesus saves! Do you know him as your personal Savior? What does it mean to be saved? Saved from what? Saved to what? How does it happen? The questions come thick and fast. Too often the answers are glib and slogan-like. But look at some of the aspects of salvation identified here. It is assumed that salvation is a condition of human maturity and blessedness which is God's gracious gift to us. We shall be reminded later that it is a process now begun, but one realized fully in the future (3:12–14; see Rom 5:10). At this moment Paul emphasizes that it always makes demands on us. It has to be actualized, achieved, worked out (v. 12). Because it is given to us, paradoxically we must work for it. But as in the Parable of the Talents/Pounds the reward of that faithful service is opportunities for additional service! That is what salvation is all about—not a privilege to be enjoyed, but a service to be performed!

Moreover, he adds, it's not to be a source of superiority feeling and smug satisfaction that provokes the rivalries and ambitions referred to above. On the contrary, we are saved in "fear and trembling" realizing that we can fail and be lost (v. 12 and compare 3:13 and 1 Cor 9:27), "lest after preaching to others I myself should be disqualified." There is a sermon there against a view of salvation as irresistible and automatic! There is no way in which we can assert our rights or lay claims upon him who saves. "All this is from God, who through Christ reconciled us to himself and gave us the ministry of reconciliation (2 Cor 5:18)." So why the inflated ego and pompous behavior?

Indeed we work in the realization that it is God who works with us and through us. He is the supreme will-er and worker (v. 13). All that he does is done "for his good pleasure," that is done for the sake of his will and purpose for humankind. That word *eudokia,* "good pleasure," in v. 13 is the same word found in the Gloria in Excelsis hymn of Luke 2:14. Thus it is that the apostle often describes the work of ministry as a collaborative effect with God, the chief minister, who chooses to make us partners.

"Earning Salvation" may be pardoned as an overstatement that might be shock therapy against salvation claims that regard it as a reward for good behavior or a privilege to be enjoyed at someone else's expense. These are perversions of the biblical understanding. Salvation, the process of "being saved," is synergistic: we work and God works to make it operational.

Here and elsewhere Paul talks of salvation not in purely individual terms but in reference to a new life lived in relation to others. The sphere is not the solitary self but the corporate life of a community. It is indivisibly personal-social, a condition of well-being that realigns all our relationships and brings about a common life "in the Lord." Every gift from God, including salvation, is a power to be employed in service to the needs of others (see 1 Cor 12:7; 14:12). Such a dynamic, developmental, and social understanding of salvation—authentically Pauline, I believe—is a far cry from the subjectivism and escapism with which it is sometimes confused. Small wonder that the salvation preaching of the church is regarded cynically, even derisively, by outsiders. Our pulpits must help people experience salvation as "Freedom From The World" interlocked with "Responsibility for The World." Two sermons there; neither of which can stand alone. The one without the other is a distortion of the truth of redemption in Christ.

"God the Enabler" might develop the theme of God present in our world (Emmanuel) not simply as Presence but as Power at work through his people. Recall the word of the Johannine Christ, "My Father is working still, and I am working" (John 5:17). Note our readiness in worship to adore, praise, and glorify God as a passive object outside our world to be contemplated, rather than a helper of the weak and a champion of justice inside our world to be celebrated. Mary's song praises a worker God (Luke 1:46–55).

The Christian Paradox: Happiness in Tribulation (2:14–18)

Carry on your mission; do what you know you should do. The appeal continues. It was bad faith for the Israelites in the desert to grumble and complain about their plight, he had reminded the Corinthians (1 Cor 10:10). Perhaps with an allusion to that story, the apostle urges the Philippians not to succumb to nit-picking and skeptical questioning—a poor substitute for concerted action. It might be posted as a reminder when church committees and boards meet for deliberation! Sometimes the way to kill a program is to open it to unlimited debate.

Then in the familiar imagery of light and darkness he summons his friends to be lightbearers in a world of shadows, holding forth the word that gives life. Thus they become God's true children instead of disobedient children in the midst of a warped world (see Deut 32:5, the Farewell Song of Moses). "Became" is to be preferred to "be" the children of God, as it is in the identical phrasing of the Prologue Hymn to the Gospel of John (1:12). Throughout the NT, the emphasis is on development, becoming-in-process, rather than being-in-status. Moreover it is interesting to note that the Johannine play on "light" and "life" is also found here and only here in Paul (compare 2:15, 16 with John 1:4). Of course we are not to understand "word of life," used only this once by Paul, as a reference to the Holy Scriptures. The Philippians were not distributing copies of the OT, and the NT was not yet written! Word of life means the gospel, the good news of salvation in Christ preached by Paul, received by the Philippians, and now, in their partnership in mission with him, shared by them with others.

That word functions as light to banish darkness and to foster life. Once again it is significant to note the intimate connection between becoming God's children as a family and acting as light bearers in the world as his delegates. His people are always his messengers. Christian existence means mission. The church exists for the sake of the world not for itself — if we are to take this description of the children of God seriously.

"Conserving Energy" may be an appropriate word to our time of energy crisis, but it must be clear that it is natural resources not human resources we have squandered and must now learn to conserve. We have wasted natural energy and, too often, failed to put to use human potential. If the church is true to its calling it will be busy turning on the lights, redoubling its efforts in its proper mission, strengthening its evangelism, enlisting new people, widening the circles of participation in its work. It is proper for Christs' people to talk about "Expending Energy." There are unlimited reserves to draw upon.

Paul's imagery shifts to the sphere of priesthood and worship as he faces frankly the likelihood of his own death in relationship to their witness. To Roman friends he had once interpreted the new life in Christ in liturgical terms as a living sacrifice offered to God. Our whole lives are an act of worship

(Rom 12:1), as he puts it, and he himself as a minister-servant in priestly service presenting Gentile converts as an offering to God (Rom 15:16). In the passage before us, the Philippian Christians are said to perform a priestly service offering their faith to God in the midst of a hostile world, as the Romans were enjoined to do (see Rom 12:1 and 1 Pet 2:5 where the church is boldly defined as a holy priesthood offering spiritual sacrifices). In such priestly ministrations the apostle views his own death as a sacrifice crowning that of his friends (v. 17). It is offered to the God of their salvation, as they offer their faith, as a service which, it is presumed, will advance his purpose in the world. So there is no cause for grief, only for mutual joy (v. 18).

"Broken Vows and Partial Commitments" might signal the easily-made, easily-dissolved arrangements of a generation that can no longer accept vows of life-long commitment. Pope John Paul II has talked about this attitude of tentativeness in terms of present day clergy. "I want out" is the easy recourse to avoid facing marital problems today. And many church members would seem to favor short-term discipleships, reviewable upon request! Put all that against a deliberate commitment "till death do us part' like Paul's, and we stand ashamed and dismayed. We need to take a long look at relationships and commitments and human worth.

Pastors concerned to open up new dimensions of meaning in the ministry of the laity can find in the liturgical language of this entreaty a New Testament base for recognizing the whole congregation as ministerial, priestly, and missional in nature. Passages like 1 Pet 2:9 and Rev 1:6 carry the same emphasis. Some sermon subjects to be explored: "People and Priests"; "The Priesthood of All Believers" interpreting Luther's concept from the NT perspective.

A Valuable Ally in Team Ministry (2:19–24)

Now to some matters about travel plans and visitation. It is the apostle's hope that his beloved co-worker Timothy, his dear son in the faith, can soon visit these friends in Philippi as Paul's representative. Paul himself needs the encouragement of knowing that harmony has been restored in the congregation. The implication is that this trusted colleague can be counted on to help to that end. Again we hear reference to other workers whom Paul might send but won't, because they are more concerned about their own special interests than the welfare of the congregation (v. 21; see 1:15a, 17). Timothy, however, shares Paul's own devotion to these brothers and sisters in Christ, with no stake in personal ambitions nor other ulterior motives. Vacillating in his own expectations about the outcome of his upcoming trial, Paul speaks at one moment of resignation to a sentence of guilty (2:17), in another, of acquittal (1:25–26; 2:24).

It is worthy of notice how Paul evaluates his team mates. They are joined with him in common cause, namely the proclamation of the good news of God's salvation. Christ is being proclaimed. Rejoice in that! But how and to what end? Some do it out of genuine love for others who need that gospel (1:16), as ministers 'who really care about you" (2:20 TEV); hence about the cause of Christ among them. Others are speaking the same welcome words but are primarily concerned about themselves and their status (2:21). Once again we hear reiteration of a favorite theme: authentic ministry is not a disguised effort at self-realization, but a wholehearted putting of oneself at the disposal of another's need. The basic question is not: what's happening to me and mine through this work, but what's happening to the congregation? He never asks whether he himself feels fulfilled, but whether the church is edified.

Are we to imagine that this is a peculiarity of the church leadership only? Or are we being exposed here to something that affects every person not just the pastor? "Marks of Valid Leadership" or "Whom Can You Really Trust?" suggest themselves as topics to be pursued in distinguishing between true and quack ministry, the statesman from the politician, the caring parent from the domestic autocrat or even the absentee landlord. There certainly are other qualifications to be considered, but nothing more important than what Paul touches on here: *he really cares about you*. Without that, none of the others count for much.

A Loyal Church Worker (2:25–30)

Once again we readers become aware that we're reading over someone else's shoulder. The intended recipients knew full well that Paul was responding to a loving act of theirs through one of their church members, a certain

Epaphroditus. Later we shall hear that these friends had collected a gift of money and sent it by their delegate as a contribution to his support and a symbol of their concern (4:14–18). Now we hear that the messenger has only lately recovered from an illness that has prolonged his stay. Paul is anxious to have him return home to relieve the anxiety of his friends, for they had learned how sick he was, and to ease his own mind about the state of the church.

It is evident that Epaphroditus is highly regarded as an associate in the work of Christ. He is spoken of as a brother, a co-worker, a comrade in arms, an accredited envoy of the congregation, one who has performed true service to the apostle's need, i.e., a minister (v. 25). He had literally gambled with his life in making contact with this state prisoner and sharing in the continuing ministry in Rome which Paul is directing still. Those are terms of honor and affection. Welcome him home "with wholehearted delight" (v. 29 NEB), as one who with you is "in the Lord."

That is an oft-repeated and disarmingly simple phrase for Christian fellowship. But it labels a whole new environment. Elsewhere when Paul talks about the new kinds of relationships between husbands and wives, parents and children, masters and slaves, he signifies them as *"en kyrio*, in the Lord."* A clue to what that means for him may be found in II Cor 5:16 where he declares that "we (Christians) regard no one from a (mere) human point of view." The presupposition is that each must be seen as a brother, each as a sister for whom Christ died (1 Cor 8:11, 12). That's the new angle of vision of those "in the Lord." The reunion of the returning messenger with his own people in Philippi will certainly be in the joy of good friends, but of the special sort that distinguishes those who share fellowship with the Lord.

There are always people who are hesitant about going home because they fear they will not be welcome. Recently Roman Catholic churches held a day of special masses for those who had left the church or let their participation lapse. Former communicants were invited back. The response in numbers surprised many priests and congregations. They did not realize how many were waiting for a friendly invitation in Christ's name to come back home. Happy is the congregation that knows how to restore fellowship to those who have become separated from it. The simple instance of this caring congregation at Philippi suggests guidance through preaching on the opportunities we must not forfeit in making real homecomings possible. From members-in-good-standing to the disaffected prodigal—all deserve to be joyfully welcomed home in the assurance that God himself rejoices over their return (Luke 15). "Outgoings and Incomings" or "This Church Specializes in Home-coming Celebrations" might be sermonic subjects. Through the centuries the problems of the "lapsed" have troubled the conscience and divided the response of the church. Are they gone and forgotten? Are they gone, but not forgotten? Are they gone, anxiously followed, joyously welcomed?

Telling Your Own Story
(Philippians 3:1–20)

Gospel Revisionists (3:1–3)

Many scholars are convinced that the canonical letter to the Philippians is really composite, made up of two or more letter fragments. We can readily understand that if we read 3:1 with NEB: "And now, friends, farewell; I wish you joy in the Lord. To repeat what I have written to you before is no trouble to me, and it is safeguard for you." That certainly sounds as though a note is brought to conclusion and reference made to a previous letter or letters. Still, one can translate 3:1a in another way: "Well then (or, as to what remains), continue to rejoice in the Lord." Of course there is in 3:1b a reference to other correspondence which may have been lost, or, as others argue, may be preserved in fragment in 3:2–4:1. In any event it is unquestionable that we are dealing with Paul's own words, whether originally part of this particular letter or not.

He wants to talk about a problem previously discussed which has to be faced continually in the churches he has helped to establish. Anyone familiar with his stinging attack in the Roman, Corinthian, and Galatian letters on leaders whom he believes are perverting the gospel, will not be taken aback by the outraged tone and abusive language directed against these Jewish-Christians or Jewish sympathizers in Philippi (see Rom 2:28–29; 2 Cor 11:16–33; Gal 5:12; 6:12–15). It is doubted that they are Jewish missioners, as some hold. Whatever their convictions and motives he views them with u most contempt (Dogs!); peddlars of bad news, not the good news (workers of evil!). Why? Because they insisted that the Gentile convert must become a full proselyte to Judaism before one could qualify for the messianic salvation available through Christ. That, for Paul, was not a minor doctrinal dispute. It struck at the heart and center of the gospel. It violated the basic Christian experience of finding acceptance by God not because of pious rites and deeds, including the ancient covenantal sign of circumcision, but solely through penitence and forgiveness. The true circumcision is not broken flesh but a broken heart (see Rom 2:25–29; Col 2:11; Jer 4:4; 9:25, 26). To preach otherwise is to preach revisionism, a different and disfigured gospel. Harsh language for dangerous doctrine!

Genuine faith always manifests itself in visible ways. Responding to the needs of other persons; a daily life of integrity and decency; joining with the community in corporate acts of prayer and adoration—these give expression to and, in turn, nourish a deeply inward life in the presence of God. But they can become formalized, structured into patterns of ethical and liturgical rules that can be performed without affecting the inner self significantly. The forms of religion, Scripture reminds us, can be preserved without the godliness they once enshrined. And the believer imagines that the charitable deed or the holy rite alone suffices to ensure communion. The temple may be full and yet forsaken (Luke 13:35).

But the spiritually sensitive in Israel recognized the need to internalize these devotional acts. Prophets and psalmists criticized a liturgizing of the covenant which obscured the reality of a broken and contrite heart as the true sacrifice acceptable to God. Now this latter day son of Israel insists to Roman Christians, many of whom came out of experiences with the complex rituals of Hellenistic religions, that spiritual worship requires the total self to be offered to God as a living sacrifice, not some animal victim (Rom 12:1). He cautions worship enthusiasts at Corinth that the central ritual acts of baptism and the Lord's Supper are not self-operative guarantees of salvation (1 Cor 10:1–5). The attitude of the worshiper and the moral outcome determine the value of the ritual act. Who are the true covenant people, God's own folk? he seems to ask the Philippians. Those who "worship God in the spirit, whose pride is in Christ Jesus" rather than trusting in any pious practice or moral achievement of their own (v. 3). An alternate reading is "worship, or serve by the Spirit of God" (see Rom 2:29 and John 4:21–24).

Out of these observations can emerge a series of sermons on the nature and function of worship, the vital center of any congregational life. The pulpit ought to be the source not only of leadership in worship but also of the continuing reinterpretation of these corporate acts of adoration and thanksgiving.

"Learning How to Sing the Doxology" might invite the consideration of worship as the adoration and praise of God rather than the self-centered celebration of our own feelings and achievements which it often becomes. "Worshipping God in a No-God World" can distinguish the Christian life over against the secular life that makes no place for the transcendent. "Religious Substitutes for Faith" suggests the way we permit creedal forms, denominational differences, the "loveless legalism of Sabbath church-going" (R. Niebuhr), the recitation of the rosary, or perfunctory prayers of confession to justify us before God and lay our claims upon him. That truly, shockingly, makes religion the enemy of faith. To do so is to nullify the gospel of acceptance by divine grace through faith. We ourselves become "the evil workers" Paul castigates.

A Personal Case History (3:4– 14)

Lest anyone suspect that he is only speculating and theorizing, Paul validates his convictions about the gospel and faith by telling his own story. The gospel of the new life through faith in Christ which he preaches is a lived and living experience to which he can testify. Listen, he says, If anyone thinks there is security to be found in heritage and personal accomplishments, I can assure him that I take second place to no one on *that* score. In race and lineage as a Jew I have whatever special advantages there are in being a member of the chosen people. Not only that, I became a model of piety and virtue (see Gal 1:13– 14), even to championing the cause of Judaism against its apostates. In my zeal for the Law I became a persecutor of the church (v. 6). But all these privileges, advantages, and achievements I discovered were utterly worthless compared to knowing Jesus as Messiah, experiencing the righteousness that comes, not from the Law through obedience, but from God through faith (v. 9).

Righteousness based on Torah obedience is a human accomplishment, he contends, that results in a fraudulent sense of security and confidence. Authentic righteousness is not the result of our own good deeds which win God's approval, but a personal integrity and a good standing with God which he alone makes possible. So it isn't something we purchase but something given to us. Our security is not in ourselves and what we can do, but in God and what he can do for us. Our sufficiency is not in ourselves but in God who suffices. That's his story. And that's what happened when he gave up everything in which he had formerly found security. Christ became the ground and center of his life. Through faith in him he found a new and genuine righteousness, not a self-achievement but a divine gift he had only to accept. His whole life now finds meaning and hope in terms of his relationship with Christ. Nothing else matters. Nothing else offers new possibility. Nothing else grants security. A core statement of justification by faith is contained in v. 9. Righteousness based upon Torah obedience is played off against righteousness through faith, that is, the righteousness from God. For Paul that new righteousness involved forgiveness of sins, a power that enables us to combat and subdue sin, and a relationship of acceptance with God. It is not a moral achievement secured by the performance of religious duties, as he had once thought, but the undeserved gift of God who forgives, and restores us into fellowship with him. The text invites a sermon on "From Rejection to Acceptance," an exploration of the essential meanings of righteousness—justification put in modern language and related to contemporary experiences of rejection and acceptance.

As any personal relationship, his life in Christ is a process of expanding knowledge, making life adjustments, iden ifying more completely, coming into closer communion. He elaborates this in vv. 8–10. It is to know Christ (vv. 8, 10), to gain Christ (v. 8), to be found in him (v. 9), to be made his own (v. 12). Note the alternation of active and passive verbs. The single and supreme gain is to know and be known, to find and be found, to gain and be gained. "I press on to make it my own, because Christ has made me his own" (v. 12). Knowing, finding, securing, owning—what is this? No theoretical knowledge about the messiah and his work. "Knowing" means intimate fellowship with Christ, sharing in his sufferings, dying in his death, empowerment through his resurrection, eternal life with him (vv. 10–11). Nothing else counts beside this. Everythings else is garbage! (v. 8). That's food for scavenger dogs, he may imply, but it's not fit for the children of God. Everything about his new life is rooted and grounded in Christ.

"Securities for Insecure Times" is a subject that might
explore the false reliances of our own security-hungry society. "Winning and Losing" borrows the marketplace imagery
of this passage to consider the win/lose character of human
existence and a Christian understanding of what is the dura-
ble asset.

There is a kind of morbid preoccupation with death and
dying in our time. In contrast consider how Paul relates
death and suffering, here and elsewhere, with resurrection
(v. 10; see Rom 6:5–11). Life in Christ is participation in his
life of poverty-obedience, his sufferings, his death, his triumph. Death is not seen as termination but entry to a new
life, "dead to sin and alive to God in Christ Jesus" (Rom
6:11). "Coming to Life" is a subject for preaching development that could explore this paradoxical truth of life
through death, both physical and existential. The movement
of the discussion is surprising and significant—he *first* mentions the power of the resurrection, *then* fellowship of the
suffering. We reverse the order. It may not be accidental but
intentional, as though to say we cannot enter into Christ's
suffering and death apart from the assurance of resurrection-life.

It is because of our new life in Christ that we may arouse
the sarcasm, insult, opposition of the world. It is the presence of resurrection-life which elicites the threats of death.
Darkness strives to crowd out light. The true disciples become vulnerable on that very count. "Becoming Vulnerable
for Christ's Sake" is a way of describing the inevitable risk,
not guaranteed success, of the Christian life. Paul Ricoeur
has written, "Saint Paul . . . invites the hearer of the word to
decipher the movement of his own existence in the light of
the Passion and Resurrection of Christ." That's what it's all
about.

The passage before us is of paramount importance in emphasizing Paul's understanding of the process, the developmental character of Christian experience. Once and again he
rejects the notion of the Christian life as a state or stage or
completed condition. "That I may *come to know* him and the
power of his resurrection" (v. 10) recognizes partial knowledge and anticipates an eventual complete knowledge. This,
with repeated disavowals of having attained perfection or

having won the race and obtained the prize, is countered with assertions of pursuing, "straining forward," "pressing towards the goal." The new life for him is always fulfillment and promise, beginning and ending, our realization and a hope. He thinks in terms of infants and adults, of baby foods and mixed diets (1 Cor 3:1–2; Eph 4:13–15).

In the present case it is conceivable that he is responding to specific claims of some who believe they have come to a state of complete knowledge and spiritual perfection. We know this was one of the problems dividing the church members in Corinth and it developed into the elitist pretensions of Gnostic Christians. Such delusions of grandeur have been a feature of spiritual excesses in the Christian community through the centuries, dubbed by Paul Scherer as the phenomenon of becoming starched before one has been washed. "Growing Up in Christ" is a theme that could emphasize the heuristic character of all our knowing and believing and behaving. It could explore the meaning of *benefiting* from our history without being *controlled* by it—"forgetting the past" (v. 13). It might reflect on the tragedy of arrested development in both personal and congregational life. It should stress the need for a goal-oriented existence, setting goals and directing action as crucial to discipleship in every day. Another sermon on, "Handling Our History," based on v. 13, might consider (1) the need to remember our past: the Christian story; our national history; our personal story; (2) the need to forget: not being conditioned and controlled by the past; (3) the new future and its possibilities which God offers.

What is this goal, the prize sought after so desperately? A recurring symbol used here and elsewhere is "the upward call of God in Christ Jesus" (v. 14; see Eph 4:4; Heb 3:1; 1 Pet 5:10). V. 11 suggests that it is the "resurrection from the dead." That too is a symbol found elsewhere, for example in Luke 20:35, and we have already met the concept in 1 Thess 4:16c. To us it seems that what the apostle and other NT writers intend to say is this: In Christ God calls us to share his own life, his gifts, and his work in the world. So intimate is the association between the Christian and the Lord that one may be said to "share his sufferings," share "in his death," and experience the "power of his resurrection" (vv.

10–11; similar phrasing in 2 Cor 1:5; 4:10–11; Rom 8:10–11). Paul has said it all, simply and tellingly, in his assurance to the Thessalonian Christians: "Thus we shall always be with the Lord" (1 Thess 4:17). Sharing in the life of the risen Christ in the here and now, brought to fulfillment in the there and then—that is the end of it all.

A sermon might be developed on the insatiable human urge to get something for nothing, rewards far beyond investment. Cereal company gifts, publishers' sweepstakes, and lifetime securities are offered in exchange for green stamps, proof-of-purchase coupons, and lottery tickets. As I write, a metal mania is sweeping the country. One coin dealer describes the panic buying in a graphic comparison, "In 1978, I did $750,000 worth of business. In the last couple of weeks, we've been buying (and then reselling) $100,000 worth of precious metals each day." Jesus and Paul also talked about rewards and prizes. Are these, then, carrot-on-a-stick enticements to encourage good conduct? All of them are extravagant gifts that are unearned, to be sure. But God's prize is not to be confused with Santa Claus gifts. It doesn't wear out; if anything it wears us out. It doesn't tickle our vanities; rather it withers them. It doesn't relieve us of work and put us at ease. Instead, as the faithful servants in the Parable of the Pounds/Talents discover, it increases responsibility, heightens the trust, expects even more from God's investments entrusted to our care. But it means true life, finding our real selves, a "more authentic situation in being." That's Paul's testimony.

On So-Called "Liberated" Christians (3:15–20)

Paul has told his own story of finding and being found, of reaching yet not fully grasping, of his deepest hope that his life may be conformed to the passion and the resurrection of Christ. As a discerning pastor he recognizes that not everyone understands that account of the Christian life in exactly the same way. There are differences in insight and outlook, certainly differences in the way the truth is grasped and expressed. Not that the pluralism is to be understood as encouraging differences of opinion or each making up his own theology. Paul would be the last to legitimate divergent views of the gospel. But he does recognize that in the community there are various stages of growth represented in understanding all that the gospel means and in living out the gospel day by day. He calls for development toward maturity: "Let those of us who are mature be thus minded" (v. 15). He believes that on every level, further enlightenment is to be sought and will be given: "God will reveal that also to you" (v. 15b).

Christian perfection cannot be understood instantly and completely (though some imagine they have a monopoly on it). Nor can the application of that insight be fully realized in our way of life. But the Christian is called to make conduct consistent with the truth as it is grasped and to stand together with friends in the common task (lit. walk in line, i.e., with others, v. 16).

"Grow up!" is the injunction. "Act your age," he advises. There isn't room for make-believe in Paul's repertoire. Professing a faith cannot be divorced from making a life, else a Christian is counterfeit. Impersonations are not called for; only the real things. "Hold true to what you have attained" (v. 16). With that Pauline appeal, one might correlate the salt-sayings of Jesus at the point of his warnings about adulterated salt (Matt 5:13 and parallels). Is the church for real, with honest people honestly responding to the heavenward call of God, or is it a masquerade party, concealing real persons under disguises? "Make-believe Discipleship" might be a sermon title exploring the deeper meanings of that text in 3:16. Similarly one could consider the meanings of maturity, rising out of the text in 3:15 under such a title as "Coming of Age in Christ."

It is by no means clear whom the apostle has in mind in the stern reproach he expresses in vv. 18–19. We may doubt that he refers to those mentioned earlier who go out of their way to be spiteful to him (1:15–17). Nor will it seem likely to many that they are to be identified with the conservative Jewish Christians he tongue-lashed earlier in this section (3:2). Perhaps he has in mind other members of the Christian community who give lip allegiance to the Lordship of Christ but use their new found freedom in the light of hope as a rationale for flaunting matters of morality. They're nominal Christians who can recite the formulas of faith, pay their dues, staff the committees, but insist on the privacy and freedom of their personal lives as the privilege of those who have been set free in Christ.

Anguishing over them, the apostle sadly calls them "enemies of the cross of Christ" (v. 18) who are on their way not to salvation but destruction, whose "minds are set on earthly things." They are Christians who are still deriving their standards and values not from the gospel but from the world. Gratification of the senses is paramount in their way of life.

How relevant all this is to our own time and society is not hard to see. In an essay contributed to a recent book on *The New Class* (ed. by B. B. Briggs, 1979), Daniel Bell profiles the new society in the western world in these terms. "It has to do with cultural attitudes, the most dominant of which in the western world is the idea of the antinomian self: the individual, not an institution, is the source of moral judgment: experience, not tradition, is the source of understanding." Political scientists and sociologists talking about the antinomian self! Autonomy, rule by the self, rules made up by the self, spells anarchy, the break up of society. It is the responsibility of a prophetic pulpit in our day to explore the deterioration of a common ordered life by self-oriented, Me-centered ways of life. It means ruination wherever it prevails; inside the church, within society, personal existence. "Narcissus or Christ", Scripture confronting Greek mythology, dramatizes the fundamental antithesis of two ways of life: that of self-indulgence and that of self-sacrifice.

Against all that, where are the models and the dominant concerns of the truly faithful? Paul sets them out in this same passage in a relief sharpened by this contrary behavior. Who are the friends who affirm rather than deny all that is signified in Christ's death on the cross? With surprising candor Paul appeals to his friends in Philippi to follow his own example. They are to model his presentation of the gospel and imitate his own behavior pattern (v. 17). They are to stand together with all those who so comport themselves. Has he succumbed to the ego-centrism he is quick to criticize in others? Is he building up membership for a Paul party? Opinions differ. But the alleged conceit should be read in the light of a passage like 1 Cor 11:1: "Be imitators of me, as I am of Christ" (see 1 Thess 1:6; 2 Thess 3:7, 9).

For Paul there is a new ego-self: "no longer I who live, but Christ who lives in me" (Gal 2:20). And we have already seen that he is not under the illusion that his life is already transparently Christ's. He is well aware that there is some distance yet to go before he lays claim upon full maturity in Christ. But he is unabashed to urge his friends to behold Christ through him.

With few support systems available we need to look for models of discipleship, always uneasy at the thought that others may be accepting us as models of Christian existence. A literary critic in a Sunday feature section raises the question, "In films, where have all the heroines gone?" It may well be asked and by no means limited to heroines. Paul is well aware of the need to teach "by precept and example," while we may wish to confine attention only to precept. Christian preaching should help worshippers reflect on the unconscious influences we exert as parents upon children, teachers upon students, older brothers and sisters upon younger children in the family, leaders upon associates. *Imitatio Christi* became very early the way to holy living. Martin Luther's word on becoming Christ to your neighbor restates the Pauline position. An invitation to the theme might be given in the title, "Where Have all the Heroes and Heroines Gone?"

Not only on a personal level are models needed. They are required also for social change. And the passage before us presents one in a striking way. The little assembly of Christians in the Roman colony of Philippi are reminded that they are citizens of another commonwealth than that of Rome, a *politeuma* that is another world entirely, yet one that already exists in this present world in the form of the church (v. 20). For the church is an advance copy, a sneak preview, of the heavenly reality (see Gal 4:26).

Numerous sermonic possibilities on the theme of the church could be precipitated out of the realization of the church as the model of the new society, God's world, an outpost of another homeland. Think of what it might mean in church life to act as an experimental center for the practice of peace and reconciliation among the estranged, the extension of forgiving love among the lovelorn and dispossessed, the branding of wrong in society as wrong rather than keeping quiet. Think of Christians as an advance guard staking out God's future in the midst of humankind's present.

"Double Passports," a sermon based on v. 20, might deal with the double citizenship of Christians in society. They exercise the rights and responsibilities of political citizenship (Rom 13:1–7), but their primary allegiance to the heavenly commonwealth relativizes every other relationship.

It is clear that Paul conceives the coming change to be all-encompassing, resulting in the total transformation of this experienced world. It is more than personal transformation, though it is certainly that. Salvation, which for him is characteristically a hope, a future to be realized, will be collective, bringing to fulfillment all history, personal and social, in the complete triumph of Christ. Then it will be that all human existence, on-again off-again in its present acknowledgement to its true Lord, will be completely ordered by his purposes and restored to his dominion. Caesar's dominion will become God's dominion.

At this point Paul anticipates that radical transformation from "our lowly body" into "his glorious body" by the miracle of his power (v. 21). Body, *soma*, always carries with it the meaning of selfhood. We capture Paul's meaning when we understand the change from "the body of our humiliation" to one like "the body of Christ's glory" to refer to the radical transformation of a weak, death-prone self into a transcendental self akin to that of the glorified Lord. Paul is content simply to call it a spiritual body (see 1 Cor 15; 2 Cor 5:1–9). While this is expressed here solely as a hope, elsewhere it is defined as a process of change already begun in the life of the believer. Just as "we shall bear the image of the man of heaven" (1 Cor 15:49) so also it must be said "we *are being changed* into his likeness from one degree of glory to another; for this comes from the Lord who is the Spirit" (2 Cor 3:18). What is now begun, is continued and will be ended with him. Thus we shall be forever with him (1 Thess 5:9, 10); "we are the Lord's" (Rom 14:8).

The whole scheme of salvation in Paul's comprehension of the gospel appears in summary in the section vv. 9–21:

(1) The new righteousness from God (not from the law) through faith in Christ (v. 9)

(2) The cruciform character of life in Christ; existence shaped by the Passion and Resurrection (vv. 10, 11)
(3) The life in Christ as quest and possession (vv. 12–14)
(4) Sharing with others now in a new commonwealth of God's design (v. 20)
(5) The hope of transformation into the image of Christ and sharing in God's eternal dominion (v. 21)

Homiletical possibilities are quickly generated by the text as we open ourselves to its leading. "Saved to What?" directs attention from the over-emphasis upon rescue *from* to liberation *into* as the real center of the Christian experience of salvation. With Moltmann we may recognize the church as an eschatological reality, a disclosure of God's future into our present, more than the outcome of past events. "What's Ahead?" could reflect on alternate futures for humanity, man-made or God-designed. "Can Human Nature Be Changed?" might be the topic for a sermon on a modification of human behavior far beyond what behaviorists dream of, the transfiguration Paul encodes in the symbols "body of lowliness" and "body of glory." To be Christ's people is to belong to Christ; is to become like him. That takes a major change. But it can and will happen, on the promise of Scripture and the evidence of changed lives.

"Minor Alterations" may serve to remind us that the change Scripture speaks of is not to be confused with the rearrangement of society's furniture when a new house is called for. Or applying band-aids when surgery is needed. Indeed even alleged change in Christ cannot simply be claimed beyond questioning. For unless the fruits of the Spirit are manifest in the "changed life," unless it is clear that one becomes more and more formed in the image of Christ—and that means visible marks of Christ's own attitude toward outcasts, inherited traditions, opponents, depressed and again delirious disciples—unless there is an authentic *imitatio Christi*, it is alteration not change. Not everyone who cries "Lord, Lord . . . "!

Workers' Conference
(Philippians 4:1–23)

Healing Some Estrangements (4:1–3)

If we accept some view of the composite character of this letter in its canonical form, then it may be said that in v. 2 or even v. 1b we pick up the main letter which was interrupted by a later insertion of a letter fragment, 3:2–4:1, between 3:1 and 4:2. In any event 4:1ff. contains a variety of exhortations to the congregation after the familiar practice of Paul in drawing a pastoral letter to a close.

We cannot   istake the evidence of the affection the apostle has for these people. Brethren, my brethren, he calls them, my beloved, my brethren whom I love, my joy and crown (see 1 Thess 2:19). They are to establish themselves firmly "in the Lord" (v. 1), that oft-repeated summary sign he gives for Christ-centered being, a Christ ambience as it might be called.

Now, at the end, he makes bold to specify some of the difficulties imperilling the unity of the congregation, alluded to several times earlier. Are these two women he names guilty of the rivalry and conceit warned about in 2:3? It is possible. Now in a direct way the apostle appeals to Euodia and Syntyche to be of the same mind (the same expression in 2:2, see 1:7). The attention given to their estrangement suggests that they hold sufficient status in the church that members of the congregation may be siding with each, whatever the dispute was about. A split in the church was threatened. It is more interesting still to note that Paul recognizes them as valued co-workers who with a certain Clement and others are registered in the book of life among the names of God's faithful. These are words of high praise.

Paul is concerned enough about the situation that he makes direct appeal to them, and also asks the intervention of another leader to bring about a reconciliation. We cannot be sure whether his proper name is Syzygus, which can be literally rendered "yoke-fellow." The apostle has worked previously with the three of them in starting the church at Philippi. He has concern for the persons involved and for the whole group. It is hard to imagine that in a letter to the whole congregation Paul would suddenly address an unidentified person simply as "you, my loyal comrade."

It takes a church squabble in first century Philippi to give twentieth century readers a valuable insight into the role of women in the churches of this time. He mentions four workers among a larger group, two of them women, who have shared Paul's labors in the cause of Christ and whom he can praise as highly as Jesus did his own associates (see Luke 10:20). Paul cannot be labelled an anti-feminist, pure and simple. The key role these women play in the Philippi congregation obviously goes beyond serving on the altar flowers committee or spearheading the rummage sale. The admittedly difficult passages in 1 Cor 11:2–16 and 14:34–36 must be read in the perspective of his commendation of the deacon Phoebe of Cenchraea and greetings to other women associates in the work (Rom 16); his rejection of a double marital standard (1 Cor 7); and his vision of sexual parity in Christ (Gal 3:28). A sermon on "The Battle of the Sexes" might examine male and female rivalries in modern society and the Pauline appeal to mutual caring in joint service to the one Lord (Eph 5:21).

Straightening Out Our Priorities (4:4–9)

"Take joy in the Lord always. Let me say it again: Be joyful" (v. 4). With that summons to gladness, the concluding portion of the letter begins. For instance, he says, the Christian community should be marked by a special gentleness, a considerateness in interpersonal relations, that is practiced not only within the fellowship but with *everyone* ("to every person", v. 5; see 2 Cor 10:1). The community is not to practice caring simply on itself, but should extend it to the families next door, down the street and across the town. "Where Do You Draw the Lines on Caring?" might explore the way we incline to put limits on love, whereas the gospel declares the unbounded, unconditional nature of holy love manifest in Christ and the mark of authentic belonging to Christ. If we love those who love us, what is special about that? "Not Genuine Without This Trademark" might explore the distinguishing signs of true rather than counterfeit church. Among others on the list, sharing, considerateness, and kindliness, ought to rank high.

Know that the Lord's coming is near (v. 5b). Don't be ridden with frettings and worries. The implication is that they are to live secure and confident in the knowledge that God is in charge (see Matt 6:25–34; Luke 10:41). Rather than going about in danger of a breakdown for fear that God has forgotten them, they are to share all their interests and concerns, little and big, in prayer-communion with the Father (v. 6). Trust in the parental care of God will dissolve all their fussings and frettings.

Prayer is not simply to be a shopping list of requirements, however. The simple but critically important phrase "with thanksgiving" distinguishes a disposition of life which Paul flags again and again. Check out Rom 1:21; 14:6; 2 Cor 1:11; 4:15; 9:11, 12; Eph 5:20; Col 1:3; 1 Thess 2:13; 2 Thess 1:3. Regularly and insistently making known our requests is a petitionary prayer that brings to mind the old Dutch schoolmaster who was said in morning prayers to lay down the law daily to the Almighty. Paul believes that thanksgiving is to be *part of every supplication*, "in everything" (v. 6). It is no after-thought. If prayer is offered in the context of the gratitude that in everything God can work for the good of his children, then our requests are framed in a different way. We are not to set God's agenda for action, but to seek help in the grateful remembrance of divine favors in the past and assurance of continuing care in the present and future.

Sermon themes leap out of a text like that. We do need guidance to help us move into the higher levels of prayer. And the sermon can provide the necessary direction and encouragement. Worrisome concerns about ourselves and others spill over from our anxiety lists and become the substance of prayers, sometimes the only kind of prayers we pray. Of course we must cry for help in our helplessness, light in our darkness. But grateful remembrance of help formerly given, grateful realization that there is a dependable Ally who will not fail us, can silence the desperation and grant peace.

We have reflected earlier on the meaning of God's peace, the heaven-born *shalom* that makes possible blessedness and hope amid our human frights and fears (v. 7). Its source is God himself. It comes from God to us. It goes far beyond anything our reasoning can do in an effort to control our failings and withstand the threats from without. That holy peace is indeed of far more worth than all our human reasoning ("passes all understanding," v. 7). It is a protective power that surrounds all of us frightened folk, guards us from the dangers that beset, and establishes us in the fellowship of Christ (v. 7b). It is truly the bridge over troubled waters.

"Not as the World Gives" could entitle a sermon that evaluates the various peace proposals that offer their wares to a war-frightened world: the easy political promises, the jockeying for power, the stockpiling of arms—all that allegedly constitutes the guarantees of peace in a world without peace. In counterpart the biblical understanding of *shalom-eirene* is presented, not to be confused with the peace-of-mind tranquilizer of secular thought, but as the wholeness of personal and social being made possible by reconciliation with God. A comprehensive well-being in God such that the absence of worry and even of war are only fragments of the whole.

It would be a legitimate summary of the whole paragraph vv. 4–7 to describe the traces of holy peace in human life as: joy in the Lord; gentleness; anticipation of Christ's victory; deliverance from fretfulness; prayers for strength with thankfulness. "Peace-Keeping and Peace-Making" would comprehend it all.

Now besides all this, says the apostle (not "finally," as RSV here and in 3:1) let me say something more. To our surprise he enumerates a number of virtues which cannot be considered exclusively Christian because they are found on many of the Hellenistic and Roman ethical lists of the day. Whatever is true and noble and just and pure and lovely and gracious, in sum whatever is of excellence and wins praise—take these into account (v. 8). Not "reflect upon" but "reckon with"—make a considered estimate of what these things are worth. Then once again the reference to earlier teaching and the example he set with the injunction: Make my way your way and you'll experience the guiding-guarding peace of God with you (v. 9).

The renowned Boston preacher, Goerge A. Gordon, used to talk about cultivating a "discriminating intellectual hospitality," by which he meant that we have the freedom and the obligation to choose carefully our literary companions. Good

books, great music, imaginative painting—these have nour-
ished humanity for centuries, broadened and gentled the
human spirit. They still offer their companionship. Why are
we still tyrannized by TV imperialism and the drug store
bookstand? Food can be found on a plate and in a garbage
pail. Are we losing the ability to recognize the difference?
Your sermon might be preached on this text under the title
"Think On These Things." This is a special kind of "Thought
Control."

In an economy where inflation rules, the prices on merchandise are in constant change. Goods may be marked up by
ten percent and more within a week. As a rule everything costs
more. Value-systems, determining patterns of conduct, are
not immune to this fluctuation. The young welcome the freedom of new values; the old mourn the loss of cherished standards of the past. How do we determine value in a society
where prices change so quickly and cost may not be a true in-
dex of quality (even the expensive things may be shoddy!). A
society where it seems as though the prices have been scram-
bled, and the merchandise is incorrectly labeled? It's old fashioned but trustworthy advice the apostle offers. Look around
and search for everything that is genuine, admirable, equita-
ble, and beautiful and stake your life on them. "Value-Test-
ing" is an obligation of bargain hunters and faithful disciples.
That's how we may straighten out a badly warped set of
priorities.

Learning How to Live Simply—and a Thank You!
(4:10–20)

Those who argue the composite character of the letter to
the Philippians usually regard this section as a fragment of
the original thank-you note that Paul wrote shortly after
Epaphroditus arrived with the gifts from the church. It
reveals Paul in a very human way, a man profoundly appreciative of the material and spiritual support of his friends, yet
somewhat embarrassed by his need of assistance, for he is a
proudly independent person. We see him fumbling to explain
that though he can take care of himself he really is grateful for
others who want to help. Few passages in his other letters
show us his sensitivities so clearly, or present him in a more
winsome way.

Take a look at the verbal images Paul employs here. There is a certain formality in the way he uses business language to acknowledge receipt of the goods (*apacho*, "I have received", v. 18); or to express their partnership with him in the gospel. "Partners in payments and receipts . . . profit accruing to you . . . my receipt for everything . . . paid in full . . . interest that keeps on multiplying"—terms from the world of business and commerce. We are reminded of Jesus' word about a divine recompense that far exceeds whatever sacrifices have been made for the sake of the Kingdom (Mark 10:29, 30). There are reimbursements to the givers out of the extravagant generosity of God through Christ that can supply all our wants (v. 19).

The secular language of banking and business becomes the imperfect means to describe loving and generous spirits, sacrificial concerns, divine generosity. Paul has a precedent. Jesus also has recourse to commercial figures in parables like the Vineyard Workers (Matt 20:1–15), the Two Debtors (Luke 7:41–42), and the Talents (Matt 25:13–30). Heavenly treasure in earthen vessels, but expressive of the way both master and disciple found a transparency in familiar, everyday experience of the humdrum world which became windows into a wide and wonderful world. It's not in flights of theological abstractions but amid the secular and commonplace that both find ultimate meanings about humanity, the world, and God's presence which otherwise go unnoticed, realities which we have forgotten existed. "Finding God in the Commonplace," is one way to say it. Or "How to Keep Life From Being So Daily."

"Your care for me has now blossomed afresh" (v. 10 NEB). Your help is welcome, but, he hastens to add, I've had to learn how to manage whatever the circumstances. For a bit he talks like a Stoic philosopher priding himself on achieving an independence from difficulties by becoming self-sufficient (*autarches*, v. 11). "I know what it is to be brought low, and I know what it is to have plenty. I have been very thoroughly initiated (a term used in initiation rites of the mystery cults) into the human lot with all its ups and downs—fulness and hunger, plenty and want" (v. 12; see his account in 2 Cor 4:8–10). But unlike the Stoic who believed he was wholly on his own, Paul's ability to cope is not of his own devising. It is strength from without that becomes his resource and support. "I have the strength for anything through him who gives me power" (v. 13).

For him, one plus God constitutes a majority in dealing with all the fortunes and misfortunes in life. One has the impression that this is not "chin up" optimism. Clichés about silver-lined dark clouds, everything will be OK, sound hollow and tawdry in the face of this deep serenity validated by long and tough experience. It is the wisdom of old age garnered at great personal cost in comradeship with Christ that finds expression here. Hear him elsewhere: "For the sake of Christ, then, I am content with weaknesses, insults, hardships, persecutions, and calamities (he didn't know then what was still to come); for when I am weak, then I am strong" (2 Cor 12:10).

The passage is inexhaustible as a resource for helping people face up to life. Is it possible that one must lose everything to discover what one really has? Is this what really constitutes the predicament of the prosperous? (Mark 10:17–23, to be re-read in relation to affluent societies which consider the greatest imaginable calamity to be the loss of fossil fuels). "Voluntary Simplicity as a Way of Life" might consider the basic gospel call to poverty. "Reorganizing Your Mental Environment" might open up new possibilities when we are unable to alter our external environments. Think what Paul and Bonhoeffer did with an unalterable prison environment. "Learning to Cope" could explore the Christian understanding of resources for dealing with adverse experiences.

There was a very special bond between these people and the apostle. Several times they had contributed to his work when he was in Salonika (v. 10); perhaps also when he was in Corinth, though he doesn't mention it here (2 Cor 11:9). And now again they have sent tokens of their love and concern. Having just spoken of his ability to do without things, he hastens to correct any apparent ingratitude by assuring them that it was good of them to share his troubles. Grateful for the gifts, he rejoices more in what they represent: an open-hearted, caring concern that prompted them to action. That's what makes them open to the heavenly blessing that enriches the givers beyond their gifts, yes far, far more (v. 19).

"Open Hands; Open Hearts" suggests itself as the title for a sermon that explores the blessedness of giving. But Paul's awkwardness in trying to say thank you points to another side of the act, namely "Learning How to Receive." From the modern missionary movement to America's foreign aid programs, there are evidences that it is often easier to give than to accept, to play the role of the benefactor in assisting the poor and the weak than to be in the humble, even humiliating, position of accepting aid from others. What is true of nations, in this instance, can be true of individuals. It is blessed to know how to receive and how to give.

Farewells and a Blessing (4:21–23)

It is time to conclude the letter. Greetings are to be given from the writers to each person in the church fellowship. No general salutations to all and sundry, but personal good wishes to each and everyone. Greetings are to be extended also from the friends and associates who are with Paul. The whole congregation at Rome sends best wishes. A special group of civil service employees asks to be remembered to them. These last call for comment. They are identified as "those of Caesar's household" (v. 22). That does not mean they are members of the emperor's family. Rather they are among the huge body of government workers, including slaves and freedmen, who manned the complex bureaucratic establishment of the empire. Perhaps some of them were Macedonians, even Philippians, and were especially eager to greet their countrymen. And with this common form of benediction, "The grace of the Lord Jesus Christ be with you" the letter is ready to be dispatched.

What may be said of the two churches referred to in this letter? Certainly they represent a variegated membership. At Rome some are taking new courage despite Paul's predicament (1:14). Some proclaim Christ but disown the apostle (1:17). Some look only after their interests and are unconcerned about the plight of other churches (2:20). At Philippi some are under the domineering influence of conservative Jewish-Christians who are strongly opposed to Paul (3:1). Some are mature, some, not so mature (3:15). Others are more secular minded than Christ minded (3:19). Two church workers are quarreling (4:2). But most are praying for the missionary pastor, anxious to share the burden of his trouble, sending tokens of their love and concern (4:14).

Yet he thinks of them all as brothers and sisters in Christ. He calls all of them saints, whether in Philippi or in Rome.

"Saints Without Haloes," to be sure, but saints nonetheless. A basic understanding of the nature of the church is reflected here which remains controversial to our own day. The church is not a community completed. Paul recognizes and accepts that. It is a community under construction, a redeeming rather than a redeemed fellowship in allegiance to its Lord, on its way to glory.

PHILEMON

Introduction: Getting Clued In

This personal note is the nearest thing we have to a private letter in the Pauline collection. Addressed to a particular person, Philemon, a well-to-do Christian of Colossae, one of the cities in the Lycus River valley in Asia Minor, it is an intercession on behalf of a runaway slave named Onesimus. We can assume Colossae as the location since it is the city of Onesimus (Col 4:9) and Archippus (Col 4:17). Not only Philemon is addressed. The apostle brings the situation to the attention also of a woman named Apphia, a certain Archippus, and the whole Christian society that assembled at Philemon's house. "In the Body of Christ personal affairs are no longer private" (T. Preiss).

An ingenious hypothesis, proposed by E. J. Goodspeed and elaborated by John Knox, regards this as the original letter to the Laodiceans (Col 4:16), channeled through Philemon to influence Archippus of Colossae who was the real master of the slave. Onesimus, Knox believes, later become a bishop of Ephesus (see Ignatius' letter to the Ephesians 1:3; 2:1; 6:2 and the martyrologies). However there is no hard evidence to support this view. We shall regard it as addressed to Philemon of Colossae, written by Paul from imprisonment, probably in Rome (AD 58–60), or perhaps from Caesarea (AD 56–58), or even Ephesus (ca. AD 55). Tacitus, a Roman historian, reports that an earthquake leveled the city of Laodicea in AD 60 and presumably damaged the neighboring cities of Hierapolis and

Colossae. The absence of any reference to this disaster in Paul's letter suggests that he is writing prior to that event. The proximity of Colossae to Ephesus (about 120 miles east) would make the apostle's proposed visit more credible (v. 22).

The Roman economy was founded on the institution of slavery. The slave population in the Empire was enormous. According to Strabo, a first century Greek geographer, Delos was the slave market of Greece where as many as 10,000 slaves were bought and sold in a single day. In the capital city, slaves and freedmen constituted the majority of the population. Many were farm laborers and household drudges, but it must not be forgotten that slaves were numbered also among civil servants, physicians, teachers, sculptors, painters, poets, musicians, and artisans of various types. Freedom might be purchased if the money could be raised. In other instances slaves could be granted the free status by an act of their owners. Onesimus was a member of Philemon's household who had run away, perhaps making off with some of the family silver (v. 18). Eluding capture and refusing the temporary safety of official asylum only to be resold, he found his way to Paul's place of detention. Befriended by the old man, he had come to share his faith in Christ (v. 10). Now he was returning home to Colossae to face the consequences, accompanied by Tychicus who was carrying a letter to that congregation and to another at Laodicea (Col 4:7–9).

Paul pleads for his new Christian friend, a "faithful and beloved brother," to be restored to good favor in Philemon's family. He must have been fully aware that the flight of a slave was a capital crime for which the slave could be seriously punished by demotion, scourging, or even crucifixion, at his owner's discretion. His request arises not out of the moral duty of humanity to slaves such as the philosophers urged. He must have known what the Torah prescribed in such a situation (Deut 23:15–16). In treating Onesimus as his official messenger to Philemon, in urging the owner to accept him as a Christian brother, as Paul does (v. 16), he might be asking both for the acceptance and the release of the slave to continue to work with Paul. The social institution is not challenged as such. Paul cannot be made into a proto-abolitionist. But a precedent is established which in time led Christian leaders to be known as "brothers of the slave" and slaves to be called "freedmen of Christ."

"As an expression of simple dignity, of refined courtesy, of large sympathy, and of warm personal affection, the Epistle to Philemon stands unrivalled" (Bishop J. B. Lightfoot). That tribute remains undiminished. Watch Paul as he deals with a delicate problem in human relationships in a pastoral fashion that involves the whole congregation.

Dealing with the Disinherited
(Philemon 1–25)

Greetings! (1–3)

A four-fold salutation from Paul and his colleague Timothy. Philemon is greeted first as a beloved fellow-worker; Apphia, probably Philemon's wife; Archippus, his "fellow-soldier," possibly their son and associate in ministry (Col 4:17), and finally the church that gathers regularly in their home. They are saluted in the same way as were the Philippians (Phil 1:2) and the Thessalonians (2 Thess 1:2). See 1 Thess 1:1 on "grace" and "peace." Paul identifies his situation as a prisoner of the state as he does in the companion letter to the whole church at Colossae (Col 4:10). Note that he foregoes his customary titles of apostle and servant of Christ and calls himself simply Christ's prisoner.

How many does Paul name as colleagues in the work of ministry? We can identify: Prisca, Aquila, Urbanus, Stachys, Timothy, Lucius, Jason, Sosipater (Rom 16:3, 9, 21), Titus (2 Cor 8:23), Epaphroditus, Syzygus, Clement, Euodia, Syntyche (Phil 2:25; 4:3), Epaphras, Aristarchus, Mark, Jesus (Justus) (Col 1:7; 4:10, 11), Demas and Luke (Phlm 23), and Philemon besides other unnamed "fellow workers." His had always been a team ministry.

One may wonder why so intimate a note is to be shared with the group that meets in Philemon's home. Is it perhaps a sly way to take the situation before the whole group and secure their support for the entreaty he makes to Philemon? Is Onesimus being commended both to Philemon and to Archippus' ministry? More likely he believes that the domestic problem involved with this runaway slave is a community concern and merits their consideration too. "If one member suffers, all suffer together; if one member is honored, all rejoice together" (1 Cor 12:26). This is not to be seen as a strictly private letter between two persons. It's a matter for the whole congregation to face.

"The church in your house" (v. 2). Not until the change of social status for the church in the imperial recognition of the fourth century are we to find formal meeting houses constructed for Christian worship. Till then folk gathered in the larger homes of members, or perhaps rented space in public buildings (Acts 19:9). These house communities were centers for worship, teaching, planning for missional activity, and, on occasion, for mapping out defense strategies. The family dwelling became the house of God. A striking example of this has been found in the third century Roman military outpost of Dura Europas. Note the references to house churches in Acts 12:12, Mary's house; the house of Prisca and Aquila, Rom 16:5; 1 Cor 16:19; and Nympha's house, Col 4:15. The little community called itself *ekklesia*, a gathering or assembly. *Ekklesia* is a secular word, referring to a political assembly (Acts 19:32, 39, 41). It was chosen by the translators of the Hebrew Bible over three hundred years before to render the Hebrew *qahal*, the *called out* people of God, as Israel knew itself, and then was appropriated by the early Christian fellowships.

One might ponder the way we today juxtapose the sacred and the secular in view of the NT practice to use a secular word to name a religious community and to regard an ordinary family dwelling house as a meeting place with God. And what of the parables of Jesus which contrive to find divine reality hidden within the common everyday experiences of life, a man plowing a field and a woman baking bread? The pulpit can provide needed help in understanding "The Sacred and the Secular." In churches that are experimenting with cell groups, fellowships and house communities within the larger congregation, it would be instructive to reexamine the phenomenon of the house church in the NT. "Small Is Beautiful" is a topic title that could lead into a sermon on the benefits and the risks in the development of small group fellowships as a form of church renewal in our day.

"Sharing Our Problems," a sermon based on Paul's admonition to both personal and social responsibility in burden-bearing, Gal 6:2 and 5 (he dares to call it "the law of Christ"), could proceed biblically with the Philemon letter as a concrete example of sharing a domestic problem with the congregational circle. This can happen constructively only where mutual trust and deep caring coexist.

Gratitude for a Good Friend and Loyal Churchman (4–7)

Paul begins with a word of grateful praise for his good friend Philemon whom he regularly remembers in his prayers (v. 4). Notice the similarity to the other Colossian letter, Col 1:3, 4. Someone, perhaps Epaphras (Col 1:7, 8; 4:12), or possibly Onesimus himself, has given a good report on Philemon's love and faith in his Lord which is disclosed in the way he works with others in the Christian congregation to which he belongs (v. 5). To love Christ is to love Christ's people, as the writer of the Johannine letters insists repeatedly. But to speak of love and faith directed to "all the saints" as well as to the Lord Jesus is not characteristic of Paul. Accordingly it has been proposed to limit the object of "faith" to Christ and relate "love" to the Christian saints. Thus one might read "the love which you have for all the saints, and the faith which you have in the Lord Jesus." But this is unnecessary. Paul is complimenting Philemon on the relationship of love and faith which he has with his Lord and all the people of God wherever they may be.

The structure of the conclusion of the long Greek sentence in v. 6 admits of several translations. Does it mean that Paul prays that the sharing *(koinonia)* of Philemon's faith may serve to promote a fuller knowledge of every good thing they have in Christ? (so RSV, NEB, TEV). Or is it a prayer that the full knowledge of these spiritual blessings will spur his friend's faith to be more effective in action for others? The latter certainly would be more congruent with what follows in v. 7. I propose to read this somewhat obscure verse with E. Lohse, "May your sharing in the faith become effective in the knowledge of all the good that is in us for the glory of Christ." Paul's point is not that a shared faith will deepen our understanding of spiritual things. It is rather that Philemon's faith must become active in love and prove effective towards others. For this is what will inform his appeal on behalf of Onesimus (v. 14). So he can rejoice over this good report about Philemon who has become a source of refreshment to his brothers and sisters in the church (v. 7; see the same expression in Matt 11:28).

Philemon is a real pillar of the church. Not only does he offer his home as a meeting place; he is a leader of sturdy faith in Christ and he believes wholeheartedly in the church and what it is doing. He knows first hand what it means to have fellowship together in Christ. He understands "every good thing" which is ours for the glory of Christ. We might ask: What is meant by "every good thing?" Remember that in the letter to the Philippians Paul expressed gratitude for their "sharing in the gospel" and rejoiced that God had begun "*a good work*" in them (Phil 1:5, 6). Earlier we heard him speak of a caring concern for others in the admonition to the Thessalonians: "Always seek to do *good* to one another and to all" (1 Thess 5:15). And Philemon will be urged to do his *good deed* (in welcoming the slave), not as a duty imposed but as a privilege freely accepted. That summary term "every good thing" has packed into it a deepening grasp of the gospel, what Christian community and ministry are about, the guiding presence of the Holy Spirit in the life of the believer and the congregation. All this is his, not to hoard but to share. "Got It? Give It!"—is Paul's counsel. The great thing about this man, to Paul's mind, is that he is a blessing, a "relief from weariness" to the whole congregation. His acts of love and faith have given them new heart over and over again. We all know what it can mean in the life of a church to have a Philemon in the membership. We wish there were more of them to go around!

Again and again as we have tried to listen faithfully to these letters we have heard the missionary pastor speak of the unequivocal acknowledgement of Christ alone as Lord. With it goes the responsibility to nurture, enrich, energize (edify), the community in Christ. The two are inseparable. One cannot truly confess Christ's sovereignty without making commitment to the welfare of the congregation. Is it to say there is no true allegiance to Christ except in the context of self-less devotion to his people? But one must understand Christ's people to include, though not be limited to, the visible church. Wherever there are penitent sinners who find their help and hope in him, Christ's people are there.

In a time when private salvation is stressed, and the single self often made the measure of value, the preacher-pastor will want to take note that the NT does not know much about a solitary Christianity. The church-less Christianity experimented with in Japan and advocated in some quarters in America will find no biblical warrant. The oft-repeated key phrase "in Christ" ("in the Lord," "in Christ Jesus")—in all some 130 times in the Pauline letters—on closer examination turns out to be a way of saying "in the body of Christ," that is, the community rooted in and governed by the Risen Lord. There is no Messiah without a people. There is no Kingdom without a people. (Ever hear of a kingdom of two, I and the Lord?). "Another Look at Churchless Christianity" provides invitation to reconsidering the biblical view of community as the sphere of God's dominion. The answer is all there in the Johannine question and command, "Do you love me? Then feed my lambs!"

"An Enduring Immortality" might entitle a sermon on the way in which people are remembered, some, regrettably, for the harm they have done, some because of heroic action at great cost, some for the enrichment they have brought to the lives of others by gifts of writing, painting, music making, some for compassionate friendships. Philemon was a man remembered within his lifetime for his loving support of others who needed it. He was a one-man support system, a force of one. More accurately, he and Apphia both brought leadership and vision to that first century church. We would be grateful to be so remembered. The question has to be put to each one of us: "How Do You Want To Be Remembered?" Let it be for good, for refreshment.

Dealing With the Disinherited: A Special Case (8–20)

Somewhat hesitantly Paul seems to come to the point of this letter. Thus far neither circumstance nor the slave have been mentioned. Now adroitly and with a certain playfulness he introduces the highly sensitive issue of the strained relations between this Colossian layman and his erstwhile slave.

Teddy Roosevelt's "Go softly and carry a big stick" comes to mind as we watch how Paul moves into action. There are quiet reminders of Paul's authority: I could command what you should do (v. 8); I am an ambassador of Christ Jesus (v. 9, though here perhaps we should read "elderly man" i.e., senior status, not "ambassador"); you owe me your very life (v. 19). But he refuses to act in any such way "for love's sake" and because he wants his friend to re-

spond not out of compulsion but of his own free will (v. 14).
With that renunciation of force come counter expressions
of love and concern. Onesimus is called his own son in the
faith (v. 10). Paul has urged him to go back home and face up
to the wrong he has done, but "in doing so I am sending a part
of myself" (v. 12). He has proven invaluable to Paul and Paul
would like to have him stay (v. 13). There is a clever word play
on the name Onesimus which means literally "profitable."
The "profitable" one became unprofitable to you, he says, but
now, as a new Christian he is truly profitable both to you and
to me (v. 11)! There is wit and charm in the way Paul introduces the name into the conversation.

So the appeal continues; the right to command is renounced. You and your family ought to welcome him back not
as a guilty slave but as a "dear brother" who needs forgiveness (v. 16). "Receive him as you would receive me" (v. 17).
Here is the heart of the matter. Paul sends Onesimus back
home "no longer as a slave but more than a slave, as a *beloved
brother*, especially to me but how much more to you" (v. 16).
There is no indication here or in v. 20 that the slave will be giv-
en his freedom and returned to Paul. Paul considers a politi-
cal-social status quite secondary to a relationship "in the
Lord." That is the bottom line of the Christian community (1
Cor 7:21–24). He argues not in terms of a Stoic or of a modern
day advocate of inalienable human rights. His is the language
of joy, love, and faith in union with Christ. To live in Christ is
to live for the community and every single member of it
whether that one is slave or free in the world.

It comes to us at first as disappointment that Paul does not
mount an attack on the vicious and despicable institution of
slavery. Why doesn't he plead the case for freeing the slave?
Why doesn't he recognize this as the paramount issue? But we
must allow for the culture-conditioning of the apostle even as
we must learn to recognize the insidious ways prevailing social attitudes and customs shape our own attempt to live as
disciples. There are many forms of slavery and political freedom, precious as it is, is no guarantee that one is truly and fully free. One may have voting privileges, and be granted equal
opportunities for employment and still be victimized by hang
ups or submit to the tyrannies of racism and sexism. We par-
rot the views of TV commentators, dutifully obey the TV ads,

ape our neighbors, and are caught up in lockstep with the rest of our society. Free? Are we really free?

The preacher has responsibility to help the congregation come to terms with the many dimensions of that cliché freedom. We need to learn how a so-called free people can experience genuine liberation. The license plate motto "Live Free or Die" can convey much more of a message than most people hear or the manufacturer intends. It is the truth of the gospel which offers bona fide freedom (Jn 8:31, 32). Paul's appeal to the whole Christian community takes on new meaning: "For freedom Christ has set us free; stand fast therefore, and do not submit again to a yoke of slavery" (Gal 5:1): "Finding Freedom"; "Christ the Liberator."

The key to Paul's assessment of persons as brothers and sisters can be found in his first penetrating realization that Christ has died for everyone so that they may come to life. On that account no one can ever again be perceived and distanced as an ordinary human being. In very fact they are brothers and sisters for whom Christ died (2 Cor 5:16a; 1 Cor 8:11). In that discovery all human estimates have been transfigured. The full impact of that could not be grasped even by Paul. He probably never recognized that the social institution of slavery was a flagrant contradiction of God's will that would have to be abolished. Like we, he was claimed and constricted by his culture. Like we, he was in process of hearing the gospel and barely perceived its challenge to cultural systems. But his world had begun to be broken apart already in the revaluation of the master-slave relationship. The slave is the Lord's freedman. The freedman is Christ's slave (1 Cor 7:22).

To declare that the new people in Christ cannot submit to ethnic, social, and sexual differentia (1 Cor 12:13; Gal 3:28) is to bring to question the social system which is based upon these discriminations. It doesn't matter whether that full consciousness has now dawned on Paul. The real matter is that he is being grasped by the gospel and the real question is Are we? I can do no better at this point than to urge the reader to hunt down the incisive essay of Théo Preiss, a French Protestant pastor-scholar, entitled "Life in Christ and Social Ethics in the Letter to Philemon," found in a collection of his papers under the title, *Life in Christ*, 1954, pp. 32–42. It is an eloquent appeal for establishing a NT base for the social message of the gospel.

A sermon on "Christian Perspectives on Human Dignity" could be developed out of the passages cited above from the Corinthian letters and brought to focus on this concrete instance in Philemon's family. Can we agree with Preiss and others that the mythological terms "rulers and powers" in Eph 3:10 and 6:12 may best be understood as symbols of corruptive cultural forces within society that disfigure human life and which are to be exposed and destroyed in Christ? (see 1 Cor 15:24 where it is said to be Christ's mission to destroy them all; see Col 2:15). Here we may well recognize foundations for a Christian social ethic. "Proclaiming Justice in the Land" declares the Christian imperative to social action, based on the gospel of Christ no less than the prophets of Israel.

"A Revolutionary Fellowship" is one way of identifying the church as a laboratory of new kinds of interpersonal relationships, as unconventional as those of a first century church in which slaves were recognized as equal with masters, all shared in the sacraments together, and identified each other not by the standards of the society in which they lived but as brothers and sisters living in a new community. How comfortable would Onesimus be in Philemon's church when he got back home? What does the Parable of the Forgiving Father in the gospel tradition have to say to Philemon? Indeed how would any runaway son or daughter, high school or adult drop out, be received in our middle class churches today? The story of Philemon, Apphia, Archippus and Onesimus and the house community to which they were attached has some pointed questions to raise about what it means to be the church in our own day.

Paul does not admit that Onesimus is guilty of larceny in v. 18. But if some of the family silver is missing and the slave is a suspect, he wants to stand surety for him. Put it on my account, he says. Then he takes the scribe's pen and inserts a promissory note, "I, Paul, write this with my own hand, I will repay the cost of damages" (v. 19a). He assumes responsibility for whatever compensation might be required legally. Thus deftly he turns the table by reminding the offended master that he, Philemon, is likewise indebted to Paul for much more than that: he owes him his very life as a Christian. It was through Paul, apparently, that Philemon became a believer. So, he concludes, grant me this favor, and gladden my heart (v. 20) as you have gladdened the hearts of others (v. 7).

A man is about to stand trial for his life. In this crisis situation he turns from his own problems to make intercession for a poor slave who may soon be on trial for his life. Instead of planning his own defense, Paul goes to considerable length to defend another victim of the social order. The preacher will recognize in this and kindred identifications with the disinherited, the friendless, and the outcast the major element in Jesus' own ministry and reflect anew on the familiar words, "As you did it to one of the least of these my brethren, you did it to me" (Matt 25:40). It is a major theme of liberation theology that God himself stands in solidarity with the poor and the oppressed. We look for a Superman and he comes as a Servant. We shout for a king and he appears as a peasant woman's baby.

Farewells and a Blessing (21–25)

It is time to say Good-bye. Paul does not doubt that his friend will do all that he asks and more. With the same confidence in his release from arrest that he expressed to the Philippians (Phil 1:25, 26), he advises his friends to prepare to receive him as a guest in their home (v. 22).

Greetings are extended from Paul's companions: Epaphras, Mark, Aristarchus, Demas (Demetrius), and Luke— the same persons named in the closing salutations of the Colossian letter. Only the name of Jesus Justus is omitted. It is an intriguing possibility that v. 23 read originally "Epaphras, my fellow prisoner in Christ, Jesus (Justus) send greetings to you." Epaphras was a Colossian who established the first Christian community there (Col 1:7, 8). Aristarchus the Thessalonian and Mark, like Paul, are Jewish Christians (Col 4:10, 11). It is an interethnic team of workers Paul assembled. For the final blessing see Phil 4:23.

Other intercessory appeals on behalf of disobedient servants, slave and free, have come down to us from antiquity. (See E. Lohse's commentary in the *Hermeneia* series, pp. 196–97, 201.) But this is unique in early Christian literature in its disclosure of Paul's pastoral concerns and its testimony to the transcendence of social distinctions in the new community in

Christ. Let George Bernard Shaw have his railings at Paul for "the monstrous imposition upon Jesus" Shaw believed he had made. The apostle has a way of provoking but outlasting his critics. In the final reckoning it will not be his adversaries, from Judaizing Christians of the first century to Alfred Rosenberg in the twentieth, that have the last word. That word will be spoken by the nameless folk through all the centuries who have felt his anxious concern for their welfare; who have been counseled in their own discipleship; and who have met in him Christ, the hope of glory.

BIBLIOGRAPHY

A few of the myriad studies of the Apostle Paul may be called to attention as preliminary to a specialized study of his writings for preaching purposes. Two of the best are G. Bornkamm's *Paul* (New York: Harper & Row, 1971) and M. Dibelius and W. G. Kuemmel, *Paul* (Philadelphia: Westminster, 1953). H. J. Schoeps' study under the same title is the most incisive interpretation we have by a Jewish scholar (Philadelphia: Westminster, 1961). V. P. Furnish has recently given us an analysis of Paul's teachings on four key issues of his day and ours, *The Moral Teachings of Paul: Selected Issues* (New York: Abingdon, 1979). Pulpit people will appreciate especially A. M. Hunter, *The Gospel According To St. Paul* (Philadelphia: Westminster, 1979) and L. E. Keck, *Paul And His Letters* in the Proclamation Commentaries (Philadelphia: Fortress, 1979).

Thessalonians. J. E. Frame's 1912 publication, *The Epistles of St. Paul to the Thessalonians*, in the ICC series continues to offer the careful exegete invaluable philological and interpretative help (New York: Charles Scribner's Sons, 1924). W. Neil's work in the Moffatt NT Commentary is a good combination of historical-critical and theological interests (New York: Harper & Brothers, 1950). More limited in its exegetical treatment, by the design of the IB series, is the stimulating commentary of J. A. Bailey (vol. 11; Nashville: Abingdon, 1955). Several more recent works may be noted. From a more conservative theological position, L. Morris deals with the correspondence in the New International Commentary on the NT (Grand Rapids: Eerdmans, 1959); D. E. H. Whiteley of Oxford publishes in the excellent series New Clarendon Bible (Oxford, 1969); and E. Best brings his mature scholarship to bear upon the letters (New York: Harper & Row, 1972).

Philippians and Philemon: Here, also, the earlier ICC commentary on Philippians and Philemon by M. R. Vincent (New York: Charles Scribner's Sons, 1911) deserves an important place on any brief bibliography. Even more useful to the pastor who is interested in serious study is the commentary on Colossians and Philemon by E. Lohse in the front rank Hermeneia series (Philadelphia: Fortress, 1971); it cites all biblical and comparative language texts with English translations. In Harper's NT Commentaries, F. W. Beare, *The Epistle to the Philippians* (New York: Harper & Brothers, 1959), offers a new translation and observations providing a base for sermonic development. E. F. Scott's commentary in IB (vol. 11; Nashville: Abingdon, 1955) is helpful but limited. Those interested in a Greek based commentary will appreciate C. F. D. Moule on Philemon in the Cambridge Greek NT Commentary, *The Epistles to the Colossians and to Philemon* (New York: Cambridge University, 1958).

Among the more recent books one might single out J. J. Muller, *Philippians and Philemon* (NICNT; Grand Rapids: Eerdmans, 1961); G. B. Caird, *Paul's Letters From Prison* in the New Clarendon Bible (New York: Oxford University, 1976); and J. L. Houlton *Paul's Letter From Prison* in the Pelican Commentaries (Philadelphia: Westminster, 1978). The IB commentary on Philemon by J. Knox (in vol. 11) embodies some of his distinctive views on this note as the original letter from Laodicea (Col 4:16) set forth in his *Philemon Among the Letters of Paul* (rev. ed., Nashville: Abingdon, 1959). A fascinating essay by T. Preiss on "Life in Christ and Social Ethics in the Epistle to Philemon" can be found in his collected essays under the title *Life in Christ* (London: SCM Press, 1954).